HOW ARCHITECTS GET WORK

Interviews with Architects, Clients, and Intermediaries

GODFREY GOLZEN

Architecture and Building Practice Design Guides: London

First published in 1984 by Architecture and Building Practice
Guides Ltd, 1 Lamont Road Passage, London SW10 0AH,
and distributed by the Architectural Press Ltd,
9 Queen Anne's Gate, London SW1H 9BY.

© Godfrey Golzen 1984

ISBN 0946228 09 4 (cloth)
     0946228 04 3 (paper)
All rights reserved. No part of this publication may be
reproduced, stored in a retrieval system or transmitted, by
any means, electronic, mechanical, photocopying, recording
or otherwise, without the prior permission of the publisher in
writing.

Typeset by Phoenix Photosetting, Chatham
Printed and bound in Great Britain by Whitstable Litho

Contents

Acknowledgements *iv*
Introduction *1*

Part 1 The Architects
Architects' Co-Partnership *25*
Ahrends Burton and Koralek *30*
The Architecture Shop *35*
Arup Associates *39*
Boisot Waters Cohen Partnership *42*
Building Design Partnership *47*
Campbell Zogolovitch Wilkinson & Gough *51*
Covell Matthews Partnership International *55*
John Clark Associates *58*
Conran Roche *62*
Jolyon Drury Consultancy *65*
Duffy Eley Giffone Worthington Partnership *68*
Elsom Pack & Roberts *73*
Fitzroy Robinson Partnership *76*
GMW Partnership *78*
Holder and Mathias Partnership *81*
Howell Killick Partridge & Amis *86*
Hulme Chadwick & Partners *90*
Levitt Bernstein Associates *94*
Owen Luder Partnership *98*
Michael Manser Associates *101*
Moxley & Frankl *104*
Moxley Jenner & Partners *107*
MWT Architects *111*
A. N. Other Partnership *115*
Cedric Price *118*
Richard Rogers & Partners Ltd *122*
Robert Matthew, Johnson-Marshall and Partners *128*
Rolfe Judd Group Practice *134*

James Stirling, Michael Wilford & Associates   *138*
R. Seifert & Partners   *140*
Francis Weal & Partners   *143*
John Winter & Associates   *147*
YRM   *151*

Part 2   The Clients
Capital & Counties Public Company Ltd   *157*
Book Club Associates   *160*
Harding Housing Association   *162*
Greycoat Estates Ltd   *165*
Debenham Tewson & Chinnocks   *168*
Property Services Agency   *173*
Andrew Sutherland   *177*
Trafalgar House Developments Ltd   *179*

Part 3   The Intermediaries
Peter Davey: Editor of the Architectural Review   *185*
Leslie Fairweather: Editor of the Architects' Journal   *189*
Peter Murray: Editor of the RIBA Journal   *193*
Deyan Sudjic: Architectural Correspondent,
    Sunday Times   *195*
Peter Sandy: RIBA Clients' Advisory Service   *198*

Acknowledgements

The author is grateful for the help given by all the people mentioned in this book; also to Gerald Styles and Stephen Trombley of the RIBA and to Helen Fisher of ARCUK who were helpful in providing general background. He would also like to thank Jill Gibbs, at whose house in Adelaide, South Australia most of the text was written, and Margaret Crowther who put it into publishable order.

Introduction

Reforms, unlike revolutions, do not alter things absolutely—which is why their effects are never as immediate and far-reaching as their supporters would like or their opponents fear. They reflect what is usually a cautious consensus about a need for change, which then proceeds rather slowly in order not to rock the doubters and even antagonists in the boat.

It would be hard to find a better example of this process in action than the revisions to the RIBA Code of Professional Conduct which were voted by the Council in October 1979. The situation before that time was that RIBA members were not allowed to initiate direct approaches to potential clients, to form practices as limited liability companies or to engage in building contracting or property development. They were also prohibited from advertising, an embargo which remained until November 1983. The provision regarding limited liability companies was not directly concerned with getting work, but it was obviously significant inasmuch as it prevented architects entering the commercial world. It also clearly signalled their distancing themselves from it, and the prohibition on various forms of practice promotion was part and parcel of that same attitude.

Only two years before a very similar proposal to relax the Code had been rejected because of opposition from members, and the leaders of that movement—notably Raymond Cecil and the SAG—indignantly lobbied against its revival now. It turned out, however, that the Council had judged the situation correctly. A poll of 1400 members ratified their decision in sufficient, if not overwhelming numbers. Interestingly enough the biggest majority was in favour of allowing limited companies. A couple of minor relaxations on the other hand were voted down: the ban on advertising and on participating in paid exhibitions of work was to continue.

What had happened to change things over such a short time? Shifts in attitude are difficult to pin down, but the most likely explanation was that by 1979 economic pressures were changing the shape of the profession in a much more recognisable way than had been the case two years earlier. Facing a declining workload, particularly in the public sector, architects were not convinced when Raymond Cecil wrote in *Building* (16.11.79), "The essence of the Code ... rests in the obligation of integrity, altruism and social responsibility that it lays on its members. In an increasingly materialistic and cynical society, it is more essential than ever that these values be upheld. It is also essential that those who uphold them are properly recognisable. The task of the architect in fulfilling his role to society and to the environment will be well-nigh impossible if he is in a simple commercial relationship with his client."

It was not so much that architects disagreed with these views as ideals. The feeling was that, being ideals, they were not legally enforceable. As Reyner Banham said a year later in his keynote speech at the RIBA Conference, "the tradition of both legislation and education, as practised in most countries, has been to proceed as if there were only one route to good architecture and to exclude, or even prohibit, other approaches." Even before the changes in the Code professional horses were already showing a tendency to bolt through whatever approaches had been left even half open. Raymond Cecil's article was in fact a reply to one by Owen Luder headed "Why the Fuss?" Luder pointed out that the changes would make very little difference in the real world, where the no man's land between the permissible and the doubtful promotion was already being aggressively patrolled. He mentioned the instance of an RIBA exhibition of the work of one particular practice "which was only possible because the architect met a substantial part of the cost involved." It was also no secret to those in the know that the prohibition on paying for the exhibition of work was being stretched beyond credibility in a number of ways. For instance, one highly respected magazine was known to ask for (and get) contributions to the cost of colour when it featured the work of a particular practice. Several books about individual firms were also published in the seventies, where it was obvious that some kind of direct or indirect subsidy must have changed hands because they could not otherwise have been commercially viable publishing propositions.

In the light of this confused situation, Eric Lyons struck a more responsive chord than Raymond Cecil in describing the Code as "rules of conduct that are remnants of 19th-century middle class disdain for tradesmen" which were already being widely breached in reality—and perhaps always had been. "What does the consultant architect do when he needs more work?", he asked. "Traditionally he hangs around influential street corners waiting to be picked up. He must not solicit but he can loiter with intent at the 19th hole." He went on to point out that, of recent years, "we have tolerated some significant changes—architects have books published about their individual practices and offered to the public, can give public lectures, write for the newspapers . . . and appear on TV."

Some of the debate that rumbled on in 1979–80 concentrated on the inconsistency between what the Code said and what was actually happening. There were also commentators who thoughtfully looked behind the pressures for change in order to justify it—and, incidentally, to see whether some more relevant and believable set of professional standards could be developed if the supposedly altruistic, non-commercial relationship between architect and client was to go. A case in point was an interesting article in the AJ (28.10.81) by John Carter headed "The Code is Dead: Long Live the Code". Carter pointed out that the justification for the Code was the belief that "Where the customer (the client) for a service is unable to sample the 'goods' before purchase ... he should also be able to call upon independent, disinterested and ethically irreproachable advice." This sort of argument, he said, had lost its force in the immediate post-war period because of the decline in the mystique of the professional. Today the computerate young architect with his degree from a poly no longer sees a distinction between himself and the builder with an MSC or a management studies diploma from a similar institution: and vice versa. The only problem was that the architect was bound by a Code of Conduct which placed him at a disadvantage in a highly competitive world with declining workloads.

Here again there were interesting opposing voices. Writing against the proposed changes in the RIBA *Journal*, Geoffrey Hamlyn recognised the problem of competition from non-architects but wrote that there was "a tremendous amount of work in the country for architects to which they at present have no access ... The general image is still one of a remote, elite and probably expensive professional." He thought that corporate advertising was a better solution and called idealistically for higher standards of design. He quoted W. R. Lethaby who said, "When a better architecture emerges we shall necessarily find a greater interest in it."

Unfortunately in the conditions of the 1980s few firms, especially in the provinces, could afford to wait that long. A. F. Craig, an architect from Solihull, wrote as follows in *Building Design* in November 1979: "If you need an architect to design your home, look in the local paper. You'll find plenty to choose from. They may be called architectural consultants/surveyors but does the public know the difference? Their advertisements appear month after month, so presumably someone must be ringing them up! ... It's essential that architects are also able to give an easily accessible service to the public. This ability to advertise unostentatiously is an honest way to promote our business."

Metropolitan practices faced a different set of problems, though competition from package dealers was in some ways similar to that which was provided by "architectural consultants/surveyors" on small jobs. This was particularly serious because of the marked decline in public sector work which began in the late seventies. Architects began to find themselves bidding for work against firms who had no minimum fee scale to observe and no inhibitions about promoting themselves. Admittedly architects provided higher standards of design but in those spheres too they came up against other professions who had more freedom of action. As Banham said in the lecture previously referred to ("The Architect as Gentleman and the Architect as Hustler") they found that "the Code and Standard Form of Contract severely frustrated their ambitions as designers . . . If they had been content to be merely architects there would have been no problem, but as soon as they tried to offer the range of services provided by other kinds of designers—graphics, industrial, interior, theatrical or whatever—they found they were obstructed either by the Code or by the Standard Form of Contract." This was true not only of pure design, but also of the range of consultancy services in engineering, planning, computers, building use and whatever other new ground the bigger firms were trying to stake out for themselves or to offer their clients. They were in competition, very often, with other professionals and consultants who, quite simply, were allowed to do things they were not.

Competition from these quarters had been less of a problem when the public sector was thriving because then clients were often other architects who were favourably inclined towards fellow professionals. In the private sector, however, the architect tended to have a relatively low place in most organisational hierarchies. This was thought to be because RIBA members were prevented from becoming directors of companies, and another relaxation in the Code was in this direction. Anthony Jones had already pointed out in the RIBA *Journal* that in the private sector, which was becoming increasingly predominant as a source of work, decisions about appointing architects to jobs were generally taken at director level and that it must be made possible for architects to reach this level—if not, other professionals would step into the gap. Much more important, though, was the fact that the revised Code made it possible for architects to constitute their own firms as limited liability companies. This had nothing to do with getting work, but it did confirm the move in practice from profession to business. In theory, it also allowed firms the benefit of limited liability in fending off claims, though in practice clients have continued to insist on insurance cover to over-ride any limited liability status.

Where the limited liability could confer real advantages, though, would be when architects set up as property developers as they were now allowed to do. Many had long seen the big profits made by developers and felt that they had no expertise to which architects themselves could not lay claim or to which they could not have access. Indeed it was thought that architects could do the job better—and be free to design the buildings they wanted. The American architect John C. Portman was held up as the ideal here, and when he came to speak to the RIBA in April 1982 the demand for seats was such that the meeting had to be held in a larger auditorium at London University. An exuberantly skilful designer who is also highly successful commercially, his first words must have been music in the ears of his audience. "I am a developer because I wanted to be a certain kind of architect. I wanted to do the things I wanted to do. I wanted to have a greater say in what I did and a greater control over my own future."

In the event not many British architects have become developers. Many of those interviewed for this book had considered the matter but had felt that ultimately they lacked the expertise in juggling commercial risks and site values that property development requires. It added another dimension of difficulty to the already complex business of architectural practice; furthermore the changes in taxation and the general economic climate have made property development far less lucrative than it was in the boom years of the mid-sixties to the mid-seventies. Quite a number of architects pointed out, in fact, that only a tiny minority of developers were the commercial giants of popular imagination. The assets they controlled were tiny by industrial standards. The recognition of this fact made architects less hesitant about approaching developers with schemes and seeing whether they could be made into a commercial package. Of all the speculative approaches allowed by the relaxations in the Code, this has been the most popular and the most effective.

One of the significant things that has in fact emerged from the conversations with practice partners, clients and architectural editors and correspondents on which this book is based is that the relaxations in the Code have had little direct effect so far. Few firms have successfully used what the Americans call "cold canvassing"—approaching potential clients for work—and many said they could never see themselves doing so, although the clients interviewed said they would always consider such an initiative, provided it was well presented and thought out; for instance if it was based on an intelligent analysis of what their needs were likely to be. Fewer still have established themselves as limited companies, generally because they had come to the conclusion that the administrative complexities of converting a partnership into a limited company could not in reality be offset by limited liability status: clients always looked for over-riding guarantees of some kind.

It is also thought that allowing avertising will not lead to any great departures from present practice. Some small provincial firms may try it on a modest scale to fend off competition from surveyors and "design consultants" of various kinds, but in the case of larger firms even that champion of more aggressive marketing, Owen Luder, has stated that "it will not make much difference to the large and successful practices ... their best advertising will remain their reputation" (AJ 7.11.79).

Can we see a clearer picture of the shape of practice to

come in the example of the USA? There too in the late seventies the American Institute of Architects relaxed its rules about advertising and on allowing members to have a beneficial interest in construction companies. Reporting on the situation for *Building*, the American architect Richard P. Dober wrote (4.4.80), "Architects with one exception have not launched significant advertising campaigns in their own behalf. First the media are designed largely for product-oriented firms, not consumer-service groups. Furthermore successful advertising depends on repeating the message several times and in market areas where some testing of results can be measured and ad campaigns adjusted to yield best results. The costs of such campaigns are usually well beyond the financial ability of most firms." What had changed, he said, was "the skill some architects exercise in getting to the interview stage" and though this is something many British firms also stressed as being important there is a major difference in method. "What does seem to work", Dober wrote, "is the direct mail marketing of material describing the firm, its current activities and illustrations of recently completed work. Some of these mailings . . . are as slick as the cover stories in the leading architectural magazines. The brochures are sent to a select list of potential clients . . . If the mailing list is carefully established experts say a one to three per cent response can be expected, much of which is 'solid leads, pure gold' as one architect put it."

British architects have looked at this aspect of American practice promotion with some interest. At least one British book on marketing professional services is in preparation and the American texts on the subject, notably Weld Coxe's *Marketing Architectural and Engineering Services* (McGraw Hill) are frequently out on loan in the RIBA library. However, Weld Coxe's London seminars have not been particularly well attended and one architect interviewed in this book who was otherwise highly sympathetic to Weld Coxe's approach, and had used "cold canvassing" with some success, said 90

Introduction

per cent of these ideas were not applicable in the UK—though he did think that the other 10 per cent were very valuable. Whatever the changes in the wording of the RIBA Code may say, it is likely that British architects—and their clients—will go on being used to a much more low-key approach than that reflected in yet another American text on marketing professional services, *Architectural and Engineering Salesmanship* by D. G. Cooper (John Wiley). "Keep skin blemishes under control", he advises his readers. "There are many types of facial cream that will minimise these problems. Take extra care with your neck and collar . . . The hand must, if possible be dry. A wet hand suggests nervousness." In his book, *The Image of The Architect* (Yale) Andrew Saint makes the point that American architects have always been under a lot of competitive pressure from architecture/engineering (AE) firms and other kinds of designers and that in any case salesmanship is much more ingrained in American life than it is in Britain, where "architecture is still a liberal profession and attracts people whose thoughts transcend self-interest". Saint goes on to say, "But if commercialisation continues apace that can hardly be maintained for long. If the next generation of architects cannot define some new relationship between the public and the process of building, they will lose that special sense of identity which the profession has treasured so long."

That "new relationship" is far from being defined, but part of it is the recognition that the architect is no longer a professional whose dealings with clients are above market forces. It is in this context that the most significant changes in methods of getting work are to be found. The relaxations in the Code are only part of this much larger process. In fact Peter Murray pointed out in a leader in the RIBA *Journal* in October 1980 that even as it stood architects had been much freer to promote their practices than they realised—the trouble was that they were making such a poor job of it. What the changes have mainly done is to clear away some of the debris that has lain in the way of working towards a new relationship with clients. As Reyner Banham put it, "One might propose that what has been done is only a piece of necessary adjustment to operational realism: that the Institute and the Architects' Registration Council have finally recognised that the day-to-day business of commissioning, designing and building those large lumps of real estate which we dignify with the name of architecture involves the day-to-day transgression of those proscriptions, covertly in some cases, but not always."

A much more significant influence on the way architects set about getting work are the changes which Banham here refers to in the process of commissioning buildings: the growth in selection by interview, the increasing use of invited competitions, and above all the trend towards negotiated and fixed fees rather than percentage ones.*

The architects interviewed were reluctant to talk about this last point because it rubbed on the sore point of competing against other RIBA members on a fee basis. Not one of the firms interviewed admitted, even off the record, to having done this knowingly, but fee negotiation is clearly becoming more prevalent; the assumption being that the client will go to more than one firm to establish a price. The borderline between this and "Dutch auctions"—prohibited by the Code—is obviously fairly narrow, and quite a number of the firms interviewed reported that clients had asked them to re-quote a lower price than the one they had suggested.

Their response to this varied. The majority said that they would cut their service in such circumstances—offer less for less money—though often they found this went against their grain as professionals. Others said that they would never cut their price because to reduce what they felt to be the necessary services or to compromise their design in such a way as to make it cheaper would become an inevitable source of trouble as the job progressed. Small firms accepted it as a

* "Competitive fee tendering" according to a news item in *Building Design* (25.11.83) is likely to become standard policy for the appointment of architects by the PSA.

necessary evil which they had to put up with, within reason, to get work. Some highly successful practices, however, had found that by sitting down with the client and carefully going through the brief it was often possible to make considerable economies without affecting functional requirements.

Closely related to the question of negotiated fees is that of doing speculative work for nothing or at a reduced fee. This is obviously inevitable when a practice produces a scheme to submit to a developer, in which case it is part of the promotional budget though very few firms, even among those who are marketing-conscious, have a formal budget for such purposes. At best they plan for it on an *ad hoc* basis in preparing their annual forecast, and the general feeling is that promotion of all kinds ought to take up about 2 per cent of fee income. The real costs of speculative work are, however, considerable and they are growing. The larger, more established practices report the increased frequency of invited competitions, with or without a participating developer. Although the firm or organisation issuing the invitation pays a contribution towards the costs of entry it never covers all the costs.

Smaller firms are often approached by minor developers to prepare a scheme on a purely "no cure, no pay" basis to see if planning permission can be obtained. Whether this is a good idea depends very much on the client. There are quite a lot of cowboy developers around who try to get small, economically vulnerable firms to do something for nothing and who are best avoided even if you are short of work at the time. Whatever the circumstances, firms who had been involved in work of this nature felt that you should never do more than enough that is necessary to demonstrate your expertise. If the potential client could not afford to pay a fee of some kind after that it was highly unlikely that he could fund the development either. In a more positive sense, however, identifying sites and offering speculative schemes to a client could be a powerful tool in getting work because it is the most obvious way of demonstrating your expertise. One practice, in fact, uses speculative work and stepping up competition entries as a highly effective way of combining tax avoidance, in a successful year, while casting their net out for further work.

Both negotiated fees and the increase in speculative work have been important factors in bringing architects face to face with the market-place, and this has had a much more important effect on how work is obtained than the changes in the Code. It is not, however, something the profession have generally welcomed and quite a number of the partners interviewed—especially those in the more established practices—shared the views Raymond Cecil put forward in one of his many attacks on the changes. "I am concerned", he said in an article in the *AJ* of 25.6.80, "with a progressive blurring of the line between professional service and commercial endeavour . . . the motivation of a profession is service—the motivation of commerce is profit." It must be said however that the evidence of recent years is that commercial considerations do not necessarily produce bad architecture (as witness John Portman's splendid hotels for the Hyatt Group and others) nor does high social purpose necessarily produce its opposite (as witness much of '50s and '60s housing). Perhaps such things are really the product of a climate of opinion outside the control of architects, as W. R. Lethaby implied a century ago. There are hopeful signs at the moment that developers are coming round to the idea that good design is a paying proposition; also that well designed schemes have a much better chance of getting planning permission than those which merely try to maximise the amount of lettable space and toss in a bit of housing to keep planning committees quiet.

They are also much more popular with users. One of the beneficial effects of economic adversity has been that clients, architects and users have been brought much closer together. The huge speculative schemes of the 'sixties and early 'seventies sellers' markets are relatively rare now. They have given way to much smaller projects, purpose-built for a particular user working with the architect and the developer from the very beginning. In one interesting case described in this book the client, working through a developer, had employed a firm of architects as project managers to work out and supervise a performance specification based on a study of his needs. The architect's job was to ensure that the building fitted the requirements on which the brief was based.

A similar situation can now be observed in housing. The huge and on the whole disastrous housing schemes designed and built at several removes from the people who were actually going to live in them have been replaced almost completely by housing associations, run by groups who themselves live in or near these schemes and who are aware that their success depends almost entirely on whether they can be let or sold. One architect interviewed in this book said that he adhered to no particular fashion or architectural philosophy but that he would like to design places which resembled as closely as possible what the user would choose for himself. The conditions for that are more possible now than they have been since real private clients—people who could afford to have a house designed for themselves—disappeared from the scene.

One place, of course, where such clients did appear suddenly was in the OPEC countries, especially during the oil boom of the mid-'seventies. Both directly and indirectly that period has had an enormous influence on the way architects now set about getting work. Many of those who went there found, for instance, that clients took almost nothing for granted about their practices. With a few exceptions their names were scarcely known, and they were required, in competition with other RIBA members—and architects from other countries—to set out their experience, to validate their skills, to show their knowledge of particular building types and generally to define their place in the construction market. Some of them found this process so salutary that they came to the conclusion that, tempting though the rewards were, they were simply not equipped to pick them up. For instance, one well-known practice based around three partners decided that having one of them permanently out of the country would disrupt their work in a way that even the possibly very large rewards of opening an office in the Middle East would not in the end justify. Some practices that failed to think things through in this way lost ground heavily in the UK during this period. The mix between existing and new clients is usually around 70:30 and though the 30 per cent is important, you neglect the 70 per cent on which the practice is based at your peril. Then there were problems of custom and culture which cropped up because at least some British firms were fairly naive about the social aspect of marketing themselves. One practice reported being involved in a consortium pursuing a multi-million pound contract in an Arab country. They lost it because one of the participants made the mistake of arriving for a consultation travelling economy class on a cheap night flight. The client made it quite clear that if they could not afford to travel in better style they would not be able to operate at the required level. None of the firms interviewed, incidentally, including some which had offices in the Middle East, said that they would enter the market if they were not already in it even though some very large projects were being built—as well as a growing amount of rehabilitation work on those that had been put up hastily and with inappropriate detailing and materials in the 'seventies. They cited the enormous administrative and financial strains of maintaining overseas offices, the difficulties of identifying decision makers in a totally unfamiliar economic culture and the problems of getting paid.

It would be too much to claim that the experience of working abroad where the writ of the RIBA did not run was decisive in getting practices to think about their role in marketing terms; but it was certainly influential in combination with the diminishing workload in the UK and the shift from the public sector, where many of the clients were themselves other architects, towards the private one imbued in the political as well as the economic climate with the spirit of the market economy. Even now, perhaps, few practices would use such terms as "marketing" or describe themselves as "market-oriented" (though some do). But in one way or another all the firms interviewed are looking at their activities on the basis of trying to establish just exactly what they are equipped to do and to go for work that relates to such considerations.

This can raise some uncomfortable fundamental questions about the structure of their practices, notably about hierarchies and succession. Many practices are built around one or two well-known names, and clients seem to expect that it will be those individuals who will look after them throughout the course of the job. The task of filtering in a junior partner or associate during the course of it requires a lot of delicacy, and some firms plainly find it difficult. One extremely well-known architect, senior partner in a large practice, seemed to be bombarded, during the course of our interview, with what sounded like rather minor telephone queries about more than one job in progress. Yet to bring in and nurture fresh blood is essential—always assuming the partners want the practice to survive them. One firm said quite frankly that they did not expect this to happen. Others gave the impression of living somewhat on past glories, and it must be said that the best clients are by no means unaware of that phenomenon. The trouble is that like so many branches of the arts, architecture depends on individual flair.

One way round the problem is to bring on younger members of the practice by putting them in charge of smaller jobs. For many firms, work under a certain value—in some cases it can go into six figures—is not economic. The answer may be to pass it on to a smaller practice—perhaps to a friendly ex-employee—or to allow more junior members to do it, possibly as a moonlighting occupation. The problem with the latter course, as some firms have found, is that what is a minor job for the practice can be enormously exciting for the individual concerned, to the detriment of his or her normal duties. Perhaps taking on a modicum of small jobs should therefore be considered an exercise in practical "continuing professional development".

It can also produce valuable and unexpected spin-offs. The person or organisation commissioning a small job today can turn into tomorrow's major client; or they may be a potentially important client in another role, as is the case with the one private client interviewed in this book, who was also the executive secretary of a rather large charitable organisation.

Small jobs can also turn into large ones. One of the criticisms made of the RIBA Clients' Advisory Service was that at least in the past they tended to pass on enquiries about major projects to a close-knit circle of favoured practices and that smaller firms were only given a look-in when the job itself was small. One practice however found that what was originally a referral for a £30,000 project eventually turned into a job with a seven figure contract value. The lesson here is that if you research the client you may find much more potential than the initial size of the job indicates.

The converse problem is that of very large jobs or very heavy workloads. One of the firms interviewed said they had deliberately not made a bid for some huge overseas projects on the grounds that work on that scale would disrupt the pattern of their practice. They had found difficulties in operating at contract values of over £30,000,000 because they could not find the right partner- and employee-to-client mix to handle them.

The question of finding the right size of working unit was, in fact, an important concern with larger practices. How does one get the economies of scale without sacrificing the work satisfaction that comes from the sense of personal achievement which makes architecture so deeply rewarding a profession? BDP, whose 800 employees make it the largest practice in the UK, addressed themselves to this problem back in the mid-'seventies and came to the conclusion that they should work as a number of medium-sized groups rather than as one enormous unit. The economies of scale were gained by providing centralised services—computer access, for instance, or specific consultancy in specialised areas as required. Other large firms seem to follow a similar pattern.

Getting a large job or coping with the problems of growth is something that also concerns smaller firms, and it requires planning in marketing terms. One architect interviewed said that he did not feel he wanted to practise more than four days a week—the fifth day he wanted to devote to teaching or to pursuing some other architecture-related interest that would prevent him from growing stale. Curiously enough this particular person at first said that he did not do anything at all in the way of marketing. He didn't "know how he got work". Yet it was soon obvious from talking to him that though he had no formal policy—not even a brochure—he thought a great deal about promoting his practice. All his buildings were photographed by well-known photographers—who, incidentally, sometimes provided job leads. He was a well-known lecturer and writer on architecture, in both the professional and general design press. He was active on the local amenity society circuit—another source of work, both from individual clients and a housing association. His buildings often feature in the press, and though he is a good architect one suspects there are other firms who do equally good work which receives less recognition for the simple reason that they have not given enough thought to how this can be achieved.

Another very interesting aspect of this architect's approach to practice was that he was extremely client-conscious. He kept in touch, informally, with all of them long after the job was finished, and if they moved on—he does a great deal of private work—he made contact with the new owners of any house he had worked on. When he moved offices, some years ago, he chose a location which was in the London borough which provided him with the bulk of his public as well as private sector work, thus signalling his involvement with the neighbourhood. He regarded close co-operation with the client throughout the building process as vital and spent most of his evenings with those who could not see him in the daytime. An echo of just how important this attitude is at every level appears in Laurence Olivier's account of how Lasdun was selected to design the National Theatre. "When we asked if he could agree that our committee might be of some small assistance in an advisory capacity, he declared that he would welcome any comments of any kind that we might care to make and that the relationship should surely be regarded as a partnership. He was the one for us all right" (*Confessions of an Actor*, Weidenfeld).

Keeping in touch with past as well as existing clients emerges from these interviews as an aspect of which many successful, marketing conscious practices are aware—and where others are equally aware of some deficiency. As stated earlier, 70 per cent of all work in the average practice comes from existing clients, and though "a member shall not attempt to supplant another architect" the distinction between this and a little delicate poaching is not altogether clear. Certainly if a client feels himself neglected in what is now very much a buyer's market, the risk is that he will wander off or be approached by a rival practice. One large and well-known firm, for instance, reported having read in the *Financial Times* (a paper which, along with the *Estates Gazette*, the *Estates Times* and the *Economist* is cited by many as providing valuable leads as well as general background in the work-getting context) that one of their clients was about to embark on a major project in the west of England. When they rang him he said, not without some embarassment, that he had already appointed an architect. It was not that he had been dissatisfied with the work they had previously done for him. It was just that not having heard from them for a long time and knowing their status he had assumed they were too busy.

Quite a number of firms reported that one of the disillusioning aspects of working abroad had been that it made them unable to give as much attention as they now felt they ought to their UK clients. By the same token, some newer practices said that they had won some important jobs for that reason during the oil boom. They had been able to respond rapidly to what were sometimes casual-sounding enquiries which a practice with its hands full elsewhere might not have treated with the same degree of urgency. That also emerged as an important point. Promoting the practice is not something that can be fitted into a functional compartment and hauled out as required. It is a continuing activity which begins with the attitude of the person on the switchboard, flows into the speed with which letters are answered, the punctuality with which site visits are observed and the appearance of the architect's offices and ends with the consideration of whether work is finished on schedule within the budgetary and time terms which had been agreed.

Continuing practice promotion in a direct and active sense is carried out in a wide variety of ways and somewhat surprisingly, the "lunch circuit" did not loom very large among them. A number of practices reported that a great deal of good-will could be generated by one or two really good parties to which much thought (and money) was given to every aspect from the graphics of the invitation card to the food and drink. Invitations were extended quite a long way down the hierarchy of client organisations—a wise move, to judge by the comments of the managing director of one very large firm of developers, who said he paid a great deal of attention to what his managers told him of their experience of working with particular architects. Some firms made a point of sending partners and associates on study tours with clients and one had the interesting idea of offering maintenance reports at a very modest fee on clients' buildings.

An idea which is being studied by a number of practices is that of producing some kind of annual report of their activities; the problem with practice brochures being the rapidity with which that often extremely expensive document dates. Some firms, in fact, do not have a brochure at all for that reason. Most have some kind of core material which sets out such details as the working methods of the practice, its specialist skills and consultancy services, short biographies of the partners, clients they have worked for, awards they have won and captioned pictures of their major buildings. This is then augmented, in one way or another, with material particularly relevant to the specific enquiry that has been received. Relatively few brochures, it must be said, contain information on two matters larger clients are extremely interested in: whether the buildings were completed on time and whether they kept within the budget. Occasionally too, they are written in the clotted prose of the more impenetrable architectural writing. Thus one distinguished firm of architects whose beautifully produced and expensively designed brochure says this of their work in housing: "The group has had much experience in the provision of large scale community facilities, with their demanding economic requirements and complicated infrastructure."

Another firm reports having commissioned a freelance writer to produce all their publicity material. They were worried at first that his style and presentation were over-simple, but found that clients and the media to whom it was also addressed liked it and that having a professional writer to look after this aspect of their work was very cost effective as compared to spending partner time on it.

Often, though, practices found that employing a PR firm was not as productive as they had hoped, and some described their experiences with them as disastrous. Editors too were unimpressed by the efforts of many PR firms. They produced uniform handouts which were mailed to all the media, from national dailies and consumer publications to the specialist architectural press. The fact of the matter is, though, that even within the limited range of architectural magazines the interests of individual editors, the way they use pictures and the kind of stories they cover varies widely. Ninety per cent of all handouts received, whether direct from architects or through PR firms, reported one editor, got thrown away. Yet it was not that his demands were all that sophisticated: all he wanted was one decent picture and a couple of paragraphs indicating why a particular building might be of interest to him. If that was the case he would follow it up.

Promoting the practice, whether to clients or to the media, has to be a matter of studying their individual requirements in relation to what the practice thinks it can offer. That is not something, therefore, which (at least in the opinion of this writer) can be laid down in a prescriptive, American-style text. The approach of this book is therefore pragmatic. It is based on interviews which reveal what practices actually do, what clients think of it, and how architectural writers perceive it. Its form is that of interviews from which a wide variety of approaches and attitudes emerge, from each one of which a useful lesson of some kind can be drawn. There are, for instance, techniques which large practices can learn from small ones, like flexibility in dealing with clients; which small practices can pick up from more established ones, like ways of dealing with the problems of growth; and which specialists can learn from non-specialists—and *vice versa*—like the rewards and problems of putting a large number of eggs in one basket.

None of these lessons seem to the writer to compromise professional integrity. Rather they seem to underline the point made by Reyner Banaham in the address to the RIBA which has several times been referred to. By bringing themselves closer to the client and asking more searching questions about his needs "these relaxations may make it easier to ask questions about the real business of architecture"; and, incidentally, what the real aims and strengths of your practice are.

Part 1
The Architects

Architects' Co-Partnership

Until about five years ago work just came through the post. Nowadays you have to pitch for it.

One of the reasons why ACP were in the fortunate position of having work just coming "through the post" emerges from the client list in their brochure: it includes an enviable number of government organisations in OPEC countries, in the Far East, Africa and the Caribbean. As with most practices who have made a success of working abroad, their experience and contacts in this sphere go back a long way before the boom years of the mid-'seventies. They were already involved in the post-war period of colonial reconstruction. By the same token, though, they were vulnerable as work overseas peaked at the beginning of the 'eighties, and its proportion of their total load is now down to 35 per cent from an earlier 50 per cent.

However it is still very important, both in the revenue it brings and in the resources it takes up. "Working abroad is not something you can do by halves", says Ken Dalley, the partner who set up ACP's Riyadh office and who remained there for two years while he supervised the construction of five hospitals. "We go out to the Middle East alone about three times a year in search of work. You can't do it on fleeting visits, because even with our experience in that part of the world it takes time to nurture one's contacts there. On top of that you have to have a local agent who may be an associate architect, a solicitor or accountant or just a person of influence—and sometimes one of the latter in combination with a professional of some kind." ACP have found, however, that it does not pay to offer retainers. Agents are paid either by a fixed sum or by a percentage of the fee if the job comes about through their efforts. They have also found that in most cases it is better to set up project offices abroad than to make longer term commitments.

Sometimes the questions asked by Middle East clients are of an entirely different order from those raised by clients in the UK, and coming up with an answer can require a detailed and costly preliminary study. "You can be asked, for instance, 'how much will it cost to build a 200-bed hospital, including all professional fees?' " Dalley says. "The answer to that sort of query would consist of one page of costs and twenty or more pages with a rough specification of what you can do for that amount of money. On top of that you have to sort out for yourself what the parameters of the situation are. What are the likely construction costs of which our fee will be a percentage? What kind of ACP staff are going to be involved at which level and over what period of time? Would they be working with British, local or other foreign consultants? Who else has been asked to quote?"

Like all practices who have worked abroad, ACP have long been used to the concept of fee negotiations which is becoming more and more prevalent in the UK. But they have always been flexible in the way they operate, a point which is stressed in their brochure. It says that the practice is "prepared to adapt its way of working to suit each project and the method preferred by the client. For example a project may consist of consultation or a feasibility study only, it may span from inception through design and supervision of construction to the provision of landscaping, site graphics and interior design, or it may be a turnkey operation."

This flexibility is also reflected in the way they have responded to changing social or market needs. "If you look at the work our practice has done since the war, you pretty much look at the trends in building in that time. First schools, then industrial buildings, then the big university and hospital boom. Now it's prisons and barracks—a sign of the times, perhaps."

Dalley feels that it has been the structure of the practice that has enabled them to move rather smoothly from one requirement to the next. It was set up in 1939 and the co-partnership concept makes it in essence a form of group practice, with each partner retaining an individual identity rather than merging into the whole. It is mainly the expertise that is pooled and this has been amplified by their close association with Northaw Engineering Consultants Incorporated, a firm of building services engineers who share the handsome Georgian house just north of London which serves as their headquarters. Quite often, these days, jobs come about through recommendations from other building professionals who have already been retained—and *vice versa*.

The keynote in approaching clients, though, is the wide range of skills ACP can tap. "Everybody is contributing a skill of some sort", says Dalley. In part he believes that good work is its own best publicity, but he also thinks that you cannot rely on it entirely. "It's important for partners and associates to be good joiners. That doesn't mean doing things you hate doing because it's a useful way to meet clients. It does however mean that if you're keen on golf or sailing you should join the relevant clubs and regard that as a potential method of promoting the practice. I sometimes regret having to turn down invitations to industry golf outings because I never learned to play golf."

Joining is not just a social business. There are certain non-architectural trade or professional bodies which are worth belonging to: the British Bureau of Consultants, perhaps.

Dalley recommends looking at clients' bookshelves to see which directories they keep. In certain specialist areas, belonging to the relevant associations can be an enormously valuable source of contacts and information.

27

Competitions are another possible source of work, and ACP go in for three or four of these a year, but Dalley is sceptical about their real effectiveness. "With a staff of 55 we may be the wrong size", he feels. "Competitions are best suited to small practices trying to make a name for themselves or very large ones with spare capacity. Certainly open competitions are a waste of time, at any rate overseas, and I suspect this is true of limited competitions overseas as well. Local interests always start out with an advantage."

I also suspect that the practices which are most successful in competitions have a "competition style". They subscribe to certain architectural creeds and pitch at competitions where the jurors share these creeds.

ACP, says Dalley, have never had a house style in that sense at all. It is, perhaps, this that has made their experiments with using a PR firm unsatisfactory. They simply didn't understand how to make solid professionalism noteworthy. An experiment with video was not successful either. They had a video made about the practice which cost a great deal of money but which did not turn out to be cost effective. What has been very successful in publicity terms was getting the Queen's Award for Export. They were the first architectural firm to do so and this made news at various levels, both nationally and locally. They held a press party to celebrate the event. Another surprisingly effective venture in this sphere was a book on health care buildings, written by two of the partners, Philip Groves and Sir Anthony Cox. "I would guess that's been far more effective than commissioning a book about the practice."

Spreading the activities of the practice into peripheral areas of architecture can also be a way of expanding awareness about it. ACP feel they have got a lot of mileage out of their GMW computer. Originally purchased as a production drawings tool, it is now being used in a variety of other ways:

for instance doing medical equipment layouts, producing graphic symbols, doing layouts for temporary units to house a manufacturing process. "We don't use it for doing basic design, but its speed in turning out production drawings is tremendous. The fact that we have something as sophisticated as this also impresses clients."

Currently ACP are taking advantage of the relaxations in the Code to study the new opportunities now open for working with developers—for instance they are looking closely at the Land Register for development possibilities in unused or under-used sites. They have also started doing a certain amount of speculative work with developers, but they are not keen to work without a fee or even at a reduced fee unless they know the client already. "There's one thing the changes in the Code won't alter. We still don't think that sprats will catch mackerels."

Ahrends Burton and Koralek

The one rule we have is that one of the three original partners assumes personal and continuing responsibility for each project we take on. If necessary we'll limit our workload to make this possible.

Some practices these days cultivate a kind of corporate anonymity: Yorke Rosenberg and Mardall, for instance, have become YRM and others choose a name, like Building Design Partnership, which pointedly avoids the cult of personality. Except that they are generally referred to in the profession as ABK, Ahrends Burton and Koralek are firmly based on the successful reputation of the original founders, though the 40-person practice now has six partners in all.

The practice, which began in 1961, was based on a star rating from the start when Paul Koralek won the International Competition for a new library at Trinity College, Dublin. Entering, and being successful in competitions has been an important element in their work ever since. The most recent example has been their much-publicised winning scheme for the National Gallery extension. They entered this in association with Trafalgar House, who paid them a proportion of their normal fee and financed some very striking models which were produced as part of their entry. Richard Burton thinks that such architect/developer associations will become more common, as will limited competitions. "Going in for competitions is very expensive", he says. "Though a developer doesn't pay your full fee at that stage, the understanding is that he will make up the difference if the scheme gets built. Sponsors of invited competitions also pay a contribution towards the costs of those who are invited to enter, but you have to have a reasonably good success rate—and a good deal of confidence in your work—to make it worthwhile."

ABK have both, and stress sheer design quality as the distinctive element in their work. It is partly because of this that they have so far kept away from using computers, whose acknowledged efficiency carries with it a good deal of repetitiveness in the way work is turned out. For the same reason they have decided to stick solely to architecture and not to become a multi-disciplinary practice. "It costs a lot of money to keep a multi-disciplinary team going", explains Burton. "You have to have a big fee income and that immediately creates the temptation to take on too much, including jobs you're not really interested in and can't put your heart into. We really try to stick to doing what we want to do." However, within the design spectrum they turn their hand to most things, including furniture and landscape design.

Richard Burton believes that well designed buildings bring their own reward apart from professional pride and satisfaction.

There's much more interest in design quality among developers because the recession showed that excellent buildings continued to be saleable or lettable even when times are difficult.

The lesson is also sinking in that it is as easy to go to a good architect as to a mediocre one.

Another new factor in the situation is the decline in spec-built premises as compared to buildings that are tailor-made for a particular user. "The developer in that case has to find an architect who can approach the user's needs and problems in an analytical way, not just someone who can put up a shell efficiently and cheaply."

However Burton believes that architects should not be

over-awed by the power of developers—one of many good reasons why ABK do not do speculative work for nothing. "A tremendous mystique built up around the notion in the 'sixties that developers were all-powerful chaps with unlimited resources or at any rate unlimited expertise in getting hold of money. The collapse of the property market in the early seventies showed this wasn't the case. If you look at the financial structure and clout of most property companies, it isn't that great."

ABK have, in fact, pursued fairly traditional ways of getting work. They have no organised marketing strategy. All they have is a good brochure—a folder which illustrates and describes their principal buildings, including an indication of costs. They also spend a lot of money having their work photographed, because simply having it seen is a source of jobs. For instance one of ABK's major projects in recent years, the development plan for the Cummins Engine Company factory in Scotland, came because Kevin Roche had seen and liked other things they had done.

The generosity of other architects has also been an important factor on occasion. The founding partners had all worked previously at Powell & Moya and it was through that practice they received one of their important earlier commissions, the Chichester Theological College. Powell & Moya had too much work on at that time and they shared ABK's philosophy about passing on jobs rather than taking on too much and diluting the quality of their work. Burton thinks, in fact, that British firms are more generous in that respect than those in other countries and recommends maintaining friendly contacts with previous employers as a good way for a new practice to pick up work. He has also found the RIBA's Clients' Advisory Service a good source on occasion.

He says that ABK would rather spend time, money and energy on maintaining their high design standards than on developing formal marketing policies. He does however say that they put a lot of effort into their presentations to clients.

In keeping with their policy of offering the skills of the triumvirate as a major selling point, all the preparatory work for these presentations is done by the three senior partners and they make the actual presentation together. Burton admits there are cons as well as pros to this approach. "Many clients like to see that the practice has strength in depth—that we're not just really a one-man band with three names on our banner. On the other hand there are clients who prefer to work with a single star name. I suppose the process is self-regulating. Clients who don't like our approach probably wouldn't be right for us anyway."

ABK's consistently successful record in competitions means that they have less difficulty than some in maintaining media contacts. Being newsworthy, they tend to be on the circuit when people like Sudjic (*Sunday Times*), Amery (*Financial Times*) or Gardiner (*Observer*)—and of course the specialist architectural magazines—are on the look-out for stories. Media coverage makes a significant contribution to the visibility of the practice, but sometimes jobs can come about simply through happy circumstances. Burton cited the example of the Nebenzahl House in Jerusalem, one of ABK's most interesting assignments. It was a private house built for a very senior Israeli civil servant on a crucial site just inside the city wall. For various reasons a foreign architect had to be sought, and though ABK had no connection with the country the job came to them through the recommendation of a young Israeli architect who had worked for only a short time in their office.

This was their sole venture in working abroad. Other opportunities have obviously arisen, but a conscious decision was made not to pursue them. "We decided that the investment in working the way we would have wanted to was too large. It would have meant that one of us would have had to live abroad and we felt that would have undermined the way we operate."

A practice which is based so firmly on the talents of its founders raises some of the obvious problems of succession which directly or indirectly crop up in many of the interviews in this book. Burton has an answer with which, it is fair to say, few of his peers would agree. "When we die, the practice will have to look after itself", he says. "We have no interest in creating architectural dynasties." One cannot help wondering, though, whether an instinct for survival will somehow manifest itself. As in the purely biological sense, it is one of those provisions which it is best not to leave too late.

The Architecture Shop

I'm making people aware of what architects can do for them—the problem is to convert that awareness into more worthwhile jobs financially.

Those opponents of changes in the RIBA Code of Conduct who believe that architects could do more to make a broader range of clients aware of what they have to offer would find a living, if perhaps disconcerting test of their ideas in David Baker's Architecture Shop. It is on the main road out of London to the M1 and in fact quite a few of the people who stop their cars outside on the way past are other architects. It is in the middle of a row of fairly undistinguished suburban shops with a hint of Hampstead Garden Suburb affluence. The shop window, very trim, has some drawings and lithographs on one side of the entrance and a selection of up-market DIY books on the other. Beyond that, half hidden by partitions and strategically placed filing cabinets, is an ordinary small architect's office—though it may be neater than some. "Being on view all the time forces us to keep the place neat and tidy", says David Baker, who started the venture at the end of 1981. "It's a useful discipline."

The modestly priced pictures and the DIY books bring people into the shop. They do not make money in themselves, but Baker believes they help to overcome the inhibitions most people would feel about barging into an architect's office. However he has found that not many jobs come from this passing trade—and a fair number of time-wasting callers. "We have people coming in with insects in a tin asking if they're woodworms. And among the serious enquiries there are quite a few that are too small for us to take on."

This does not bother Baker, who believes that architects should have the same kind of role and status in the community as doctors.

Carrying the analogy further, Baker gets a lot of his work through what he calls "surgery sessions". He runs these three times a week and intending clients are asked to make a booking for what is approximately a 20-minute session. That is a free service, though a fee is charged when it involves going to see a building or a site. At or after these sessions possible courses of action are suggested. Most important of all, perhaps, bearing in mind the nervousness of many smaller clients about professional charges, Baker draws up what he calls an "Experimental Schedule of Fees and Services". It bears the warning that it has been "prepared for guidance only and does not form part of any contract"; but it does give a rough breakdown of what is involved and the fees that are likely to be charged, either on a percentage of construction costs or on a time basis.

Not surprisingly, the kind of jobs that usually come Baker's way are very small by the standards of most practices. They range in contract value from £2500–£80,000, and quite a lot of them are grouped towards the lower end of the scale. But can you make that pay? The answer appears to be that in a modest way you can, provided you are geared to the architectural equivalent of bulk sales. The Architecture Shop are about to start on their 200th job in three years, and in that time David Baker's staff has grown to two architects, a part-time draftsperson and a secretary. He admits that he has never yet achieved his profit target and that his own drawings from the practice are no more than he would make as a middling employee elsewhere; but he says that despite the extra headaches, it is worth it in terms of job satisfaction.

One of the plus points of doing a lot of small jobs is that they take up comparatively little time, so you never get bored. Baker discriminates, within reason, on the basis of interest rather than fees, though each job has to cover its costs. "Apart from that we look to see if it contains some kind of technical or design challenge. Sometimes, of course, it depends on who the client is. If it's a relative or a friend or someone who might lead to more work, we'd probably take it on anyway." One of the architectural services he has consciously chosen not to provide is structural surveys, though he often gets asked to do them. "I'd really rather leave that to estate agents/surveyors and as a matter of fact we often get work as a result of passing such assignments on to them."

Another source of work is found in referrals from other architects of jobs they consider too small. Sometimes, though, they're not so small and Baker has learned to be a bit wary of some of these.

Sometimes a practice passes on jobs to a smaller firm because they're too busy—but it can also happen that the client is bad news in some way.

Despite his commitment to the concept of community architecture, quite a lot of Baker's work has in fact come through conventional channels. Some of it has come through the Clients' Advisory Service and through being on the Hampstead Garden Suburb's approved list of architects. At the moment there is a good possibility of some specialist medical design work. "That kind of thing comes through social contacts, very often", he says. "Some of them are people I've got to know through the synagogue. Then, my wife is active in the Natural Childbirth Trust, so she comes into contact with a lot of young couples that way."

The Architecture Shop has filled a need and aroused a great deal of interest from the beginning. Baker had a press launch and he got a lot of coverage, both locally and in several national magazines, and this did bring a good deal of the pump-priming work which a new practice needs to get off the ground. In a modest way, however, Baker is now facing some of the problems of growth. "I made more money in the first couple of years, working on my own and sharing an office with an interior designer, than I do now that I have a small staff to help me", he has discovered. "Taking on staff creates its own problems because you have to keep the flow of work related to staffing and *vice versa*. That means having to do something about marketing, though at the moment I'm not quite sure exactly what that should be. Making people aware of what architects can do for them is one thing—converting it into jobs which are worthwhile financially is another." He does however take the view that among his clients there are several who, in a few years' time, could be playing an important role in business or the professions. Admittedly that is rather a long-term prospect, but there are certainly worse places to look for tomorrow's major clients than among the upwardly mobile residents of Hampstead Garden Suburb.

Arup Associates

The way clients come to us is a rather mysterious process. We might nurse someone along for years without result and then an organisation we've never heard of rings us up out of the blue.

A great many people, of course, have heard of Arup Associates though some of them still tend to confuse the practice with the equally well-known firm of consulting engineers, Ove Arup & Partners. They are, in fact, connected: Arup Associates was set up in 1963 as a parallel architectural partnership for the design of buildings and to provide advice on a whole range of purely building problems: planning, building law, environmental services, cost control and contract management. Since then Arup Associates has grown into a large multi-disciplinary firm with a staff of about 130 which includes quantity surveyors, structural, mechanical and public health engineers and interior designers as well as some twenty-seven architects. There are eleven partners covering all these professions, and, as one might expect from a firm that size, most of their work is large scale, though they like an occasional leavening of smaller scale jobs as well. They are organised into multi-professional groups which are kept small to maintain tight design teams and also get some of the more personalised characteristics of the ordinary-sized practice. On the other hand they have a powerful battery of resources at their disposal by virtue of the Ove Arup connection; for instance they share computer facilities, an R & D unit, a library, geotechnics and certain other specialities like traffic and fire engineering.

Ove Arup & Partners have also been a source of clients, especially abroad, where the practice has been involved in a number of major projects. Its multi-disciplinary skills are a help there because clients like all the work to be done by one entity.

Their jobs cover a broad spectrum from a major rebuilding project in the centre of Baghdad and a master plan for Loughborough University, to designing schools, swimming pools, concert halls, industrial buildings and offices, and undertaking major rehabilitation schemes. Working on that scale and being as well known as they are creates, they say, its own momentum. They have no formal marketing policy. "We have become known for the work we have done", says their spokesman.

They do however have quite sophisticated tools for making presentations to clients, including their own lecture theatre with all kinds of up to date facilities. They also set great store on making models and getting top-notch photos made of their buildings. Exactly how these resources are used in presentations depends on how specific the enquiry is. "You can't be too precise at an early stage because you don't know what the problem is."

The ability to define those problems through an analysis of the client's requirements is something they stress in their approach. They see this as a two-way process. "The client has to arrive at an understanding of what his requirements are and we regard the briefing process as a vitally important dialogue in which we sit down with him to examine the design implications of what he wants. That may mean changes in the design—or alternatively changes in what he would like, ideally, to do. In the end, though, our role is to make proposals. It's the client who has to make the decisions." That is not an easy role, especially for the client who has not been used to working with architects. They feel it is always a good idea for prospective clients in that situation to talk to existing ones in order to arrive at an understanding of how an effective architect/client relationship can be built up.

The practice is somewhat sceptical about open competitions because that essential dialogue with the client is not available. They take a much more favourable view of limited competitions in which Arup Associates are often asked to take part. The reasons they give for that are threefold: a better brief, the fact that they are competing against practices of similar standing, and the much greater likelihood that the winning entry will actually get built.

Further indirect sources of work are winning architectural awards such as the *Financial Times* and RIBA ones. Arup Associates schemes are premiated most years, though they believe that the RIBA award engenders less publicity since the rule was established that a building has to be completed for at least two years before it can be entered. "By that time it's been shown in most of the media. It's lost the impact of immediacy."

Market research, as far as Arup's are concerned, is largely a matter of keeping in touch. Teaching and talking at conferences is an important part of that process and many members of the practice are active in these spheres. In addition not only the architects, but also the structural and building services engineers teach, assess and act as external examiners in a number of schools. This helps to keep the practice aware of changes and trends.

Unlike some firms, Arup Associates seldom turn work away, though they do concentrate on trying to get interesting jobs. One reason for that is that they help to attract and hold good staff. For an established practice that is a major concern because like most architects they believe that doing good work is the best form of publicity there is.

But though they have relied very much on traditional methods of "being known" and "keeping in touch", they have lately become aware of the fact that this may no longer be enough. The danger that rivals might step in if a firm hides its light under a bushel of professional reticence is a thought that Arup Associates are currently pondering.

Boisot Waters Cohen Partnership

Developers like working with someone who understands their language. That doesn't mean that you have to dance to their tune. On the contrary, you have more chance of getting the design solution you want if you can demonstrate that it is financially viable.

The Boisot Waters Cohen Partnership is a practice that makes no bones about offering a range of skills to attract entrepreneurial, commercially motivated clients. Though they are relatively small, with a full-time staff of five plus three part-timers, they have an impressively blue-chip list of corporate clients and tackle jobs with an average contract value of £800,000, though this has gone as high as £2.3m and they will, if required, do a £200–£300 structural survey.

With the clients they now have and aspire to in the future, Brian Waters, one of the two partners, feels that apart from design there are two professional services which it is extremely important to be able to offer. One of these is knowing your way around planning legislation, his own speciality. The other is valuation advice, and this is the *raison d'être* of his partnership with David Cohen who was a valuation surveyor with Conrad Ritblat and worked at Bovis before joining BCWP at its inception in 1972. In addition to valuation they also advise on property acquisitions and disposals, lease and rent reviews and rating appeals. Inevitably these services attract architectural work such as briefing, design, specification and contractor selection. "At one time architects used to be much more involved with valuations", says Waters. "But at some point, I don't know when, it dropped out of the palette of professional services. A pity, because the financial insights you get are quite invaluable."

This is particularly true in their case because of the amount of work they do with developers. Knowing a lot about how developers go about their business protects the Partnership from many of the hazards of dealing with them; including, possibly, an excessively respectful view of the skills and resources some of them claim to have. "Developers talk of 'using' an architect and that word often has an edge to it. They exploit architects, keeping them running around looking at sites and doing a lot of feasibility stuff for nothing. You shouldn't let yourself in for that unless there's a really good chance that something will come of it, if not with that scheme, then with another the developer might be able to put your way. But even then, you should never do more than two to three days' work on that basis. The worst disservice that you can do yourself is to put up a badly thought out scheme because you haven't the time and resources to do it properly." The important thing, Waters says, is to know your developer, because the good ones are also those that will deal with their professional advisers fairly. "At the very least he should have the land, or have the resources for that. Otherwise he's just mucking about at your expense." He also says that if you are involved in planning permission work, there should be a fee over and above that for other architectural services. It can involve months of work and if it is successful the added value of the site for the client will usually run well into six figures.

It is also important to select carefully the developers whom you approach with schemes. More and more architects are doing this, and David Cohen spends a lot of time looking for sites in the *Estates Gazette* and the *Financial Times*. Some developers now feel that architects are getting better at putting up schemes than the estate agents who had the field to themselves before the Code changes. "They just send in details of the site. Architects, at least those who are serious about this method of finding work, are nowadays sending in site plans, development analyses, minutes of discussions with planning officers and feasibility studies." Waters thinks that this in-depth approach will inevitably lead to some of the larger practices becoming developers themselves, though in his opinion it is something best left to the experts.

Though ultimately recommendations from clients are the most effective way of getting work, Waters also feels that the Code changes have completely altered the name of the game. BCWP now do a lot of cold convassing based on an intelligent reading of property advertisements, but he says that "on spec" approaches have to be based on demonstrable practice skills in the field where the approach is being made. For instance BCWP have acquired some expertise in the development of Freeports now being sponsored by the government. He has written a number of papers on the subject and done some research on it for the *Economist*—so that is where they would be looking for opportunities. They would send a short letter with their brochure, a simple but effective A4 document which gives details of the partners' backgrounds and aims, their corporate clients, books and articles they have published and a few pictures. They have not, however, found the immediate response to cold canvassing very good, though quite often it produces a result later.

Marketing, Waters stresses, is not something that can be confined to making an active pitch for work. "The architect who doesn't answer the phone or deal with letters promptly will lose out no matter how good he is in other respects. The concept of providing a service is something everybody in the practice has to be aware of, and that includes the girl on the switchboard. Being efficient and businesslike will itself give the architect more freedom with design solutions, as well as general credibility. Giving a service includes taking on jobs which don't necessarily pay off in the short term.

We're sometimes asked to do surveys for which the fee is something like a couple of hundred pounds. Not our favourite form of work, but it often comes from accountants or solicitors and can lead to bigger things for that reason.

In the course of its eleven years, BCWP have learned that it pays to be pragmatic about the work they take on. During the depths of the recession they lost a couple of important jobs. "We had to sit down and think where we could get some revenue from. One way seemed to be to write some articles which could spread the word about the practice's range of services, but which might also be of some use to editors. At that time we had an associate who had previously worked on a newspaper and it was suggested that we should focus on the Community Land Act, which we knew a bit about, having had a couple of clients who had been involved with some of its ramifications. We mapped out some synopses and sent them to the AJ, *Building* and other specialist papers." They found an instant response among editors whose readers wanted to know about the Act, but who hadn't mastered this complicated topic for themselves. The upshot has been that writing has become a regular activity for Brian Waters and a minor profit centre for the practice. He was just off to Hong Kong to write up Norman Foster's Hong Kong and Shanghai Bank, but he spends quite a bit of time on less glamorous assignments, going round the country looking at and writing up buildings.

Quite apart from the money and getting his name about, he also finds this provides a useful source of information on materials, techniques, contractors and general do's and don'ts. In the latter regard, he feels it is wise to stay within sight of what you can do. For that reason BCWP have not taken on overseas work, except in a couple of cases where they have worked as a consultant with an architect on the spot.

Writing has also given Waters a valuable insight into the

45

The Architects

way editors operate as well as a lot of media contacts. He is a great believer in press releases, but says that they must be appropriate to be effective. Architects should bear in mind that if they want to get the attention of clients, a few column inches in a national newspaper is worth a page in the specialist press. It is also worth remembering that newsworthy items need not necessarily be confined to purely architectural work. A consultancy on a major planning appeal can, in fact, be more interesting to a news editor than the design of a building.

The biggest problem about getting work, though, faces the new practice without a track record to point to. "I can't tell you the answer", says Waters. "But I can tell you the usual way: in one shape or another, it's nepotism."

Building Design Partnership

What we want to put over is that BDP *is in effect a group of medium-sized practices, each of which has a strong suit in some particular area of expertise that can be called in to help out in any situation that occurs.*

Not many practices have to face the problems of growth on quite as large a scale as BDP, though to a lesser degree they affect any expanding practice. BDP, though, are a special case. Their staff of 800 makes them the biggest private practice in the UK and possibly in Europe. Apart from architecture, they embrace 16 other design professions and their introductory brochure says that "BDP tackles all types and scales of project, from a visiting card to a regional plan." It lists eight separate offices and there are no less than 52 partners, nine of them with senior status.

This potentially unwieldy structure is broken up by giving each office a great deal of autonomy, with its own chairman and group of partners. The offices were set up on the basis of an economic survey which divided the country into 12 regions—so there is still further expansion to come. However, the ultimate direction of BDP is set by a three-man management committee. That and a package of central services in which marketing plays an important role are the main points of attachment between BDP's Preston head office and its countrywide network.

Indeed BDP's present marketing policy itself emerged from their strategy of combining centralisation with devolution. "In the mid-'seventies the practice had contracted down to 500 people", says Christopher Ratcliffe, the partner whose special responsibility is the marketing aspect. "We really

47

The Architects

thought that if we were going to get back into an expansionary phase we had to find out more about where to place our efforts and to identify our clients' needs in a way that was profitable to them and to us. Part of that exercise was to develop a strategy which looked at what kinds of work we were successfully doing now, what we wanted to do in the future and how we could get it. The starting point was to try to identify where the work was coming from—by area, by building type, from what clients into which BDP offices."

Dividing the country up into economic regions was one product of that survey, but the object of that was not purely locational. It was also to scale down operations in relation to a size clients could identify with. "The contract value of our work is anything from £50,000 to £100,000 or even £200m. But there's a danger that clients might regard a practice of our size as too big to handle a £250,000 job. We wouldn't want that to happen."

Within each office there are what Ratcliffe calls "nodes of skill" which can be called up and deployed further afield, if necessary. Conversely, each office has a list of client contacts which is available on the computer throughout the practice. "We have a list of who knows whom in any given organisation. So when information comes into our central clearing house about a new project, we can call up a specific name on a 'who do we know at XYZ?' basis. We also record contact dates. Such things don't stay fresh for ever."

Ratcliffe thinks that for personal contacts to be effective they have to stay personal.

When an approach is made, a new activity announced, a press release sent out, it's always done on a personal basis, from a named person at BDP, not just from BDP as a firm.

Marketing, though, is not just confined to announcing or promoting specific occasions and activities. There are social events, sponsored lectures, and what Ratcliffe calls "encounter lunches". The object of these is not simply to invite people from whom one hopes for work directly, but to introduce past, present or potential future clients to other practice contacts whom they might find interesting. The role of this in marketing is that it is part of a long-term image-building process.

BDP do not, however, aim to build an image by creating a specific house style. "I suppose in a broad sense you could say that we specialise in buildings that call for a highly technical performance specification—and integration of services, structure and design at a rather sophisticated level. But within those parameters we're rather flexible. For instance the BDP design for the Peak Club at Hong Kong in the Royal Academy's Summer 1983 Exhibition (a fanciful grouping of pavilions in a traditional Chinese design) is not the sort of thing most people would associate with us. But we give our designers plenty of scope."

That also extends to allowing moonlighting—small jobs that BDP doesn't want to take on are passed to staff to do in their own time. Apart from economic size the criteria on which the decision to take on or pursue a specific job are based rests on the philosophy of BDP as a whole. Though not tied to any particular design "ism" they aim for quality, social values and to reach the financial objectives of both the practice and the client. All jobs are audited to see that they meet these criteria—especially at formative and design stages.

BDP are also firm believers in the value to the practice of entering competitions. They are one of the few firms who believe in pitching for open competitions abroad, but Ratcliffe says, "Win or lose you always benefit. We were pushed out of the big international competition in Vienna in the early 'sixties, but the ensuing controversy brought us a lot of publicity and ultimately led to our being commissioned by a multi-national to do another project of almost equal value."

Despite BDP's multi-faceted marketing activities, Ratcliffe says he would find it difficult to attribute success to any one factor. "It's an overlay of a lot of different things a practice undertakes—writing, lecturing, keeping in touch with clients, getting written up in the press—they're all important. When you see something that feels like it's going to work, it's a bit like rifle shooting. You gradually zero in on the target and then you squeeze the trigger—but very gently."

Campbell Zogolovitch Wilkinson & Gough

It's essential to specialise these days, either geographically or by developing tremendous expertise in some particular technical field or building type. You've got to be the practice the client thinks of right away when a project comes up.

In comparison to most new practices, CZWG might be considered to have started life with a silver drawing pencil in their hands. The four partners were outstanding students at the AA, and certainly among those in the know there was interest in what they were going to do from the time the practice was started in 1975. In the light of that it is significant that to a large extent they have relied for their success not on winning prestigious competitions, but on the much less glamorous business of getting to know planning procedures in and around central London.

In Roger Zogolovitch's view there is, however, a strong connection between that and design quality. "Well designed and interesting buildings stand a better chance these days of getting planning permission", he says. "It's not like it was in the 'sixties when permission was given almost as a matter of course, provided the client and architect were reasonably credible. Nowadays you have to satisfy interest groups like residents' and amenity associations, politically motivated planning committees, stringent government policy on conservation, tough legislation on fire risks and so forth. You have to be able to answer detailed questions, like the performance of building materials."

Back in the 'sixties a firm like CZWG would probably have been more involved in the trendier end of public sector work than with considerations like these. But they recognised right

The Architects

from the start that the public sector was in decline and that their future lay in commercial work. Thus offices, restaurants and conversions have been the mainstay of their practice and their jobs range in contract value from £500,000 to £3.5m. As it happens working with private clients suits the partners, both because of their individualistic and innovative design style and by temperament. "We like to work with the man who makes decisions. I don't think our style would fit in with the processes of the public sector, where you can't easily get at the person who has that power—if anyone does there. It's usually done by committees."

Zogolovitch believes that getting planning permission depends as much as anything else on intimate knowledge of an area, its decision makers and information brokers. That does not mean CZWG tout for work, nor even that they conduct any concerted market research, though Zogolovitch himself is an avid reader of the *Financial Times*, the *Estates Gazette* and the *Economist*. But that is only for background. For hard information he relies on what he calls "the City tom-tom"—a network of planners, estate agents, developers, district surveyors and financiers with whom he keeps in constant touch. He gets to hear most of what is going on in CZWG's chosen parish and for that reason CZWG are often retained by developers to advise on the potential and planning permission prospects of particular City sites.

They never work for nothing, though. "Getting planning permission is a complex, long-drawn out business and the benefits to the client are enormous. It adds £100,000–£150,000 to the value of the site right away. There's no reason on earth why an architect shouldn't charge professional fees for that kind of work." Apart from anything else, it's a matter of financial necessity. Zogolovitch thinks it is a good idea for architects to open an office and pay themselves proper salaries rather than resort to expedients, like working from home at nominal wages, which hide real costs.

The awareness of costs has also made CZWG sceptical about competitions. "We've gone in for a couple and won one, but

I'm not sure it's an effective use of practice time, as far as we're concerned. It depends on what sort of practice you are, though. There are firms, like Jim Stirling's, whose work is geared towards entering and winning competitions and they're very good at it."

Somewhat surprisingly, for an architect whose cast of mind is firmly entrepreneurial, Roger Zogolovitch has great misgivings about architects becoming developers in their own right and his response to the claim by one well-known architect that making money as a developer was easy was an expletive best left deleted. "It requires a very shrewd appraisal of all kinds of risks, many of them in commercial areas with which architects are quite unfamiliar. It's too easy to get carried away by the visionary aspects of a site without taking these factors into account. But when you become a developer you take on all these extra risks and uncertainties in addition to those you normally face as an architect."

The philosophy of focusing your expertise and sticking to it takes Zogolovitch into views on the future of practice that many architects would regard as decidedly controversial. In direct contrast to those who feel that they should take a more direct role in the building process, he says, "It's the phases after the design stage that are so time-consuming, expensive and risk-laden: doing the working drawings and supervising. I think architects might find it's worthwhile foregoing the fee income on these later stages in favour of doing more design. That's what they enjoy doing and are best at."

CZWG have taken these ideas well beyond the talking stage. An article by Andrew Saint in the AJ (18.5.83) describes how they have teamed up with a developer-builder, for whom they are providing private house designs under licence. "The arrangement is simple", Saint writes. "CZWG design a house type for which they make standard drawings, a limited set of details and a layout and elevations for a given site. For this Preston [the developer] pays a fee per unit built ... The lump sum is paid over when full planning permission has been received, in which connection some further payments may be made for extra drawings. Formally the architects then have no more to do with schemes. Kentish Homes (the name of the firm involved) use their in-house people to build and supervise, keeping generally to CZWG's design but reserving the option to amend and cut corners if they can do things more simply, intelligently or cheaply. CZWG acquiesce willingly, even enthusiastically, to this arrangement. They are absolved from the tedium of supervision and argument with the builders over the trivialities of detailing."

Saint, an architectural historian, points to the parallels between this way of working and what happened in the 18th century. At worst, he says "architects, if consulted at all, just furnished a smattering of style to satisfy ground landlords and make the houses sell". At best, though, they were people like Dance, Holland and Nash who "were able to control more of the building process . . . because they had the ear of those in charge of Georgian 'building control' ".

Selling house plans to developers—and incidentally CZWG have shrewdly retained the rights outside Hackney and Tower Hamlets where Kentish Homes have an exclusive licence—would perhaps be regarded by an older generation of architects as an abdication of responsibility. But for a practice which feels itself to be strong on design, it may be a way to give ordinary house buyers a standard of design they could not otherwise afford. The market may well be ready for such a move, which would parallel that of Conran with his furniture in the 'sixties.

Covell Matthews Partnership International

A lot of people think that getting work in the Middle East is a matter of going through the princes, but they're wrong. Most architectural jobs are small change to them, unless they're minor princes, in which case they're no good to you. You have to find people who have the ear of decision-makers. They're the ones whose influence really counts.

Jerry Matthews is the voice of experience because the practice of which he is a senior partner has been one of the most consistently successful work-getters among British firms operating abroad. Like that of almost all their serious competitors, their experience stretches a long way back before the oil boom of the mid-'seventies. They began working in Singapore, Nairobi and Cairo in the early 'fifties on War Office jobs which came to them through army service contacts. Later they strengthened their position in East Africa, where they have done an enormous amount of work, by buying a controlling interest in a practice founded by Sir Herbert Baker in the 'twenties and which became, before the second world war, the practice of Jackson and May: May being the Ernst May of modern movement fame.

They continued the trend of opening up overseas offices into the mid-'seventies (Covell Matthews, incidentally, are classified by the RIBA as a "large practice" and also have several offices in the UK), when they established bases in Jeddah and Abu Dhabi. They had been active in Abu Dhabi and in Kuwait for some time and this had convinced them of the necessity of taking this expensive step. With several jobs of a contract value ranging between £1m and £25m they had a lot at stake. "You've got to hear of work coming up before it becomes common knowledge. That's the real advantage of maintaining a local office, though sometimes you hear of jobs in unexpected ways—through meeting the right person on a plane, for instance. I've never got jobs through other consultant professionals, by the way—more the other way round. It's generally the architect who gets appointed first."

Apart from supervising on-going jobs, another useful function of the firm's local offices is to keep London informed about new competitions. Competitions have caught on in the Middle East, but not many are worth going in for. When they are, the rewards of success can be considerable. CMP, for instance, have just won a very big competition for the Abu Dhabi Tourist Tower. The fact that they are on the map in this way also means that they get a fair number of approaches to enter invited competitions, though the costs of doing this are high. Matthews quoted figures of up to £70,000. You need first-class models and good perspectives to have any hope of success and because of that the client's contribution seldom covers an adequate part of the cost.

The most frequent way in which you are asked to compete, though, is on fees. "Roughly our formula is a sum based on the number and nature of the drawings and the amount of practice time these will take. We multiply these costs by a factor of 2½–3. We also try and work out some savings through arrangements with other contractors. For instance the H & V contractor can generally be persuaded to swallow the cost of his working drawings in the price; likewise the concrete contractor might be able to see ways of absorbing a certain amount of structural engineering work in his budget."

Arab clients, Matthews says, like to feel they're getting a bargain, even if it is only a small one—though he doesn't feel they're any different from British developers in that respect. But the Arabs lacked sophistication in the way they handled competitive situations in the early days of the oil boom.

"They tended to accept cut-price jobs from third world architects who in some cases weren't even properly qualified and who sometimes disappeared before the effects of their mistakes made themselves evident." The result has in fact been to the benefit of others in the area, because a fair amount of work now on the go involves putting right actual or threatened building failures from the boom years.

Otherwise, Jerry Matthews thinks that the best years of opportunity in the region are now past, though there's still plenty of work about. Surprisingly, he says that there are one or two £100m jobs around for the taking, if you have the resources in terms of people and money and are willing to take the risks involved. Nevertheless, "I wouldn't myself go into the Middle East now", he says.

One reason for that is that there is an increasing amount of competition from local firms. "Big Arab consultants get preference, which is natural enough. They tend to employ expatriates, so I see more of a future for British architects as employees than for British practices in that part of the world."

John Clark Associates

If you get a really good client, pull out all the stops for him. Always be available. Be ready to work round the clock if he needs you.

John Clark's firm, which emerged in its present shape in 1980 out of an earlier partnership he had set up with two former colleagues, relied originally on just such a relationship. They had got to know the group chief architect of the major stores group Debenhams in the early 'seventies. He had indicated that he was interested in making a change, and that he would become a client if Clark, with his two partners at that time, Roger Gould and Colin Kelly, were to set up on their own. For some considerable time Debenhams and then another stores group, Allders, were by far their biggest clients.

Later in the 'seventies, John Clark became concerned about his practice's excessive dependence on these two firms and began to cast his net wider. As a result they now also work for a number of other major clients, especially Land Securities, Arrowcroft, Bovis and McAlpine and have a close relationship with a firm of chartered surveyors. The practice now has three partners, four associates and 38 staff. Their growth has, however, been achieved by fairly conventional methods. They have never found direct approaches to clients to be successful; nor PR. "Work comes mainly from doing good buildings that get noticed by people who matter, though we do do a certain amount of entertaining of journalists and so forth. It's important to be a good mixer and keep up relevant social contacts. For instance we have a very good Christmas party to which we invite everyone we deal with. We put a lot of effort, and quite a lot of money, into it, but we don't talk business there. It's simply a way of ensuring that everyone in the practice keeps in touch with those outside at least once a year."

More recently, though, their most significant growth area has been in the Far East. Indeed it is probably fair to say that few people even within the profession had any idea of the size of the practice until their £100m Shenton Way scheme in Singapore was featured on the cover of the RIBA *Journal* in 1983; but that is only one of several very large jobs they are working on in Malaysia and Singapore.

The Far East connection came about by chance—one of the partners had worked out there and got to know some local developers—but once it was established, John Clark applied his principle of "pulling out all the stops". "You're expected to be accessible and on call at all times," he says. They go to great lengths to prepare schemes when asked to do so, and it can cost up to £50,000 for an elaborate proposal to include models, drawings and written submissions. Drawings, he feels, are particularly important when making presentations in developing countries, and his own background—he was a perspective artist when he worked at GMW—has helped here. Nowadays, though, he is mainly too busy to do the drawings himself and he employs first-rate freelance perspectivists like Helmuth Jacoby, who may charge as much as £4000 for a single drawing, as well as some in-house people. The importance of presentation drawings in their work has meant that it has been worthwhile for the practice to invest in a PMT machine which can produce reductions and enlargements.

As in Britain, the client pays part of the cost of preparatory work in making planning applications which are as important a part of the building process in the Far East as they are in the UK. The understanding is, of course, that the architect will get the job if permission is granted.

Though the local, mainly Chinese, developers are good

decision-makers, there are cultural differences that one needs to get used to.

You might visit someone over a period of months, off and on, without anything coming up—without even getting much apparent interest. Then he might suddenly push a multi-million pound scheme over to you and ask you if you can do anything with it.

For this reason he and his partners always keep in touch with potential clients there, though they have not yet found it worthwhile to open an office in the Far East. "It would cost about £100,000 a year to do that and at present it's cheaper to make regular visits. I've been over four times in the last nine months."

John Clark Associates is one of those firms who feel their main skill lies in making planning application presentations and in the pure design side and who prefer the contractor to produce the working drawings and to do the site supervision. But to get that kind of relationship to function effectively Clark says you have to work very closely with the contractor from the early stages; you also have to constantly check his working drawings with the master drawing profile to make sure that he is keeping as closely as possible to your design concept.

You also need professional clients. "With building types like hotels, offices and shopping centres you're dealing with pretty experienced people at all levels, who understand what architects can and cannot do". He also finds that such clients seldom haggle about fees. In fact John Clark says that in such circumstances he would reduce the service—to try and find a cheaper way of achieving a similar result. The bottom line, though, is design quality. "We would tell the client to go elsewhere if we felt that was likely to be compromised."

John Clark Associates' brochure is a handsome and expensive document produced in a ring binder. An ingenious assembly method means that it can be put together to meet individual enquiries without the make-shift appearance that this sometimes produces when the document is in a bound form. John Clark's own earlier experience, though, was in film-set design and this, plus the fact that his practice spends a lot of money on presentations leads naturally to the question of producing videos. "It's still very expensive— about £1000 a minute, though prices are coming down", he says. "But don't under-estimate the difficulties of producing a really professional-looking job. Though you can get the equipment relatively cheaply, making a video isn't like taking photographs. It's not a DIY thing."

Conran Roche

I've always believed in approaching clients in a straightforward way if I thought I had something to offer them. I never thought it was morally inferior to buttonhole people at golf clubs or dinners.

Sir Terence Conran is not an architect—"I wish I were", he says, but as Britain's best known designer and one of the country's most successful entrepreneurs he has the capacity to make his dreams come true. Hence he has become chairman of the new—and already significant—practice, Conran Roche. His partner, Fred Lloyd Roche was the highly regarded chief architect of Milton Keynes, and Conran Roche will follow a pattern of designing buildings for industry and business as well as housing. Conran has provided some of the finance, but more importantly he intends to apply to an architectural practice some of the marketing methods that have made his various business ventures so successful.

Sir Terence thinks that there is no great difference between what he has done and what architects could do—though he feels that even now they are deterred from marketing themselves by various self-imposed professional inhibitions. This often means that the marketing function is not carried out at all or is done badly because no one's heart is really in it. "I'm a great believer in PR, for instance", he says. "But not the mindless rubbish that's churned out by some people—roneod sheets and invitations to go on expensive junkets. You've got to give some thought to what is newsworthy—a story, a new approach to something. There really isn't any need to butter up the press with big lunches, either. You're not doing journalists a favour if you give them a story—that's how they earn their salary; and if you can't give them a story they won't publicise you, no matter how much you spend on entertainment."

The same principle, he feels, should be applied to architects' brochures. "You've got to be looking all the time for some angle that will stick in the client's memory. You seldom get a job from it right away. It happens because you've said something or illustrated something that strikes a chord much later." He thinks they should be professionally designed and written, though obviously under careful briefing. As a designer, he doesn't subscribe to the view that architects are necessarily good designers in other fields—it's dangerous to infer too much from the existence of a few all-round geniuses who were as good at graphics and furniture as they were at buildings.

In the end, though, marketing boils down to being clear about what it is the practice has to offer.

You've got to be clear what the object of your practice is when you're going out for jobs. It's perfectly OK to be a commercial practice selling the architectural equivalent of baked beans provided you do it well. But it would be fatal to go into the baked beans business if you're not that kind of firm.

His partner, Fred Roche, has already made it clear—if there were any doubt about the matter—that Conran Roche is not going to be in the "baked beans" business. In an interview with Deyan Sudjic in the AJ (27.7.83) he said. "If we were asked to provide asbestos sheds we'd say no. There would be plenty of other people to do it." Where they have seen a gap, Sudjic reported, was in "work for the growing number of developers and financial institutions which . . . are becoming disenchanted with the workmanlike but mediocre competence of the large commercial practices" but are still afraid of *avant garde* designs. Part of that process of reassurance seems to be contained in the decision on where to locate their offices: in Milton Keynes. "When our clients come here" Roche said. "They can see all around them what we have done."

Not many practices are in the position of being able to say to their clients, "If you seek a monument look around you". But the lessons of the Conran story—that there is a wider market for good design than most people ever suspected—is one that should not be lost on architects, or their clients. Whether it can be transferred from furniture and household objects to buildings is likely to be one of the most intriguing questions of the 'eighties.

Jolyon Drury Consultancy

Architects have to guard against professional arrogance to which I admit I'm not entirely immune. You have to train yourself to listen as well as talk.

Jolyon Drury takes a somewhat detached view of the profession because, although he is a qualified architect and an RIBA member, he does not regard his firm as an architectural practice in the accepted sense of the term. Its main functions, described in his inexpensively but neatly produced ring-bound brochure are "industrial facilities planning, production systems design and storage and distribution systems". These are highly engineering-oriented skills and the two partners, Drury and Derek Allcard, are respectively architecture and mechanical engineering trained, as are their two full-time staff. Drury says that everyone's roles are fully interchangeable in relation to any task on hand.

He regards himself as an architect who might equally have become an engineer, and his background means that he is often brought in by other architects as a specialist consultant. He has, for instance, been retained by Norman Foster for parts of his Hong Kong and Shanghai Bank. As far as non-architectural clients are concerned he seldom engages in what he calls "primary design". More often he is brought in on matters of development strategy, and he charges either on the basis of pre-arranged lump-sum fee or on a time basis with a ceiling.

Drury feels that it would have been very difficult for him to have made as much progress as he has had he set up as a generalist architect, though he has found his design training

65

very useful. "Being able to draw as well as to be able to do the calculations is a great asset—it's a great pity that the distinction has grown up the way it has between architecture and engineering." His guru as a man who combines these two skills in architecture and engineering is Peter Falconer, the very successful West Country architect who specialises in industrial buildings.

Drury's unusual combination of skills has stood him in good stead in another sphere. He is in much demand as a speaker and writer in this field where the introduction of automated new technology has focused almost as much attention as it has in office planning. In fact he began contributing to specialist technical magazines while still an undergraduate and could probably equally well have made his mark as a technical journalist. He had not long graduated, for instance, when he co-authored a standard book on industrial storage with Peter Falconer. His writing, he says, has been a good source of further work, as well as of income in the early days of his practice.

In a more passive mode, Drury makes a point of reading all the journals in his fields of activity: materials handling, distribution, retailing, electronics—and, of course, the *Financial Times*. That in itself is quite a time-consuming occupation, but it is one that he regards as essential.

Keeping up with the journals gives you the belly feeling of an industry. When we go in to see a client we take care to know at least as much as he does in an area which is now moving very quickly.

Drury is critical of the profession in that respect. "They often haven't done their homework before they go to see a client", he says.

The consultancy's brochure simply gives a brisk and business-like description of their activities and outlines the experience of the partners and includes some recent articles by Drury himself.

They spend more money on presentations, which Drury regards as essential for a firm offering a consultancy service. "We have several meetings with the client and they might stretch over several hours involving an overhead projector and slides as well as a lot of speaking. We don't think videos would be the right medium for that, though I can see that it might be a useful way of setting out a thumb-nail sketch of one's track record. But for anything more specific I think it would be too inflexible." The care they take over their presentations is what gives the Jolyon Drury Consultancy the edge over some much larger competitors. They obviously form a sizeable practice cost, and the question of when and whether to charge can be a delicate one because the distinction between giving advice and making a proposal is sometimes difficult to draw. It's a question of judgement as to whether such a consultation might lead to something bigger. Sometimes, on the other hand, they might provide their service at a lower price to a small client if they genuinely feel that is all he can afford at the time, and if the job is an interesting one.

Drury keeps in constant touch with clients. In his field it is particularly important to see how the solutions he has suggested are working out. Lunches are a good way of keeping in touch informally, but though a self-confessed workaholic Drury keeps lunches at his club sacrosanct. "That's where I go to relax", he says, confident in the feeling that competence is the best marketing tool he has.

Duffy Eley Giffone Worthington Partnership

We devote a lot of attention to establishing what the corporate structure of our clients is and trying to find out who makes the decisions, though this certainly isn't a line of investigation one can follow beyond a certain level. After that it's more a question of instinct and experience and picking up the atmosphere in meetings.

DEGW specialise in office planning, and that comment by founding partner John Worthington reflects something of the thinking of a practice that regards the study of the client's organisation as an inseparable part of solving his design problems. It is the product of an architectural training which in the 'sixties took three of the partners to the USA, where they were all Harkness fellows. "At that time it was the fashion over there to expose students to a variety of disciplines", says Dr Frank Duffy. "In our case we all got involved in the social sciences and their application to management. That's been the major influence on our work, though I would say that our most innovative contribution to office design has been applying city planning principles to the micro-scene."

At first, Duffy and Worthington began working in the UK for an American company, JFN Associates Space Planners. They set up their own practice, which now has a staff of 34, including 7 partners and 7 associates, ten years ago. That decade has coincided with what has probably been the most eventful period in the whole history of office design—a period during which the initially revolutionary notions of Bürolandschaft have been overtaken by the much more far-reaching impact of the new technology. This has created a continuous and growing demand for the practice's work, the contract value of which ranges anywhere between £16,000 and £6m.

One reason for this apparent disparity in contract values is that smaller jobs are in fact often commissioned within the same organisation and in doing them they regard themselves as working for a particular part of it rather than the organisation as a whole. "Working for an organisation may involve doing dozens of different jobs for different departments of the same firm who nevertheless have very little contact with each other", says John Worthington. "In getting work from clients structured in this way our analysis of organisations is very relevant and useful."

They have found, though, that the person they are dealing with in a client company always likes to feel they are getting attention from someone at senior level within DEGW. "With seven partners and seven associates out of a staff of 34, some people would regard us as top heavy, but this is partly a matter of getting as many people in the practice involved in its progress as possible and partly one of client relationships. There's always a partner or an associate involved in any job." The practice itself is broken down into a number of working units to further this aim. For instance DEGW London deals with jobs within a day's trip of London, and that includes a good deal of work in Europe. DEGW Overseas handles more distant work, though their Mexican venture, DEGW Mexico, is again a separate unit. Finally there is Building Use Studies (BUS) a research company in which DEGW has a 30% interest, of which the two active directors are a sociologist and a psychologist. They take on space planning-related consultancies—for instance, most recently, a study of coin handling processes in the Post Office.

Running the practice in this way is all part of an overall strategy of maintaining contact with clients—a matter which they regard as vital. John Worthington says, "We send them brochures, offprints of articles and news about the firm.

We're now thinking of producing an annual report for our clients—that's done quite a lot in the States."

They also keep track of prospective clients. Part of that process is simply reading the relevant journals—in their case those in the fields of management and office technology as well as the obvious professional magazines in architecture and real estate. But they consider that easily their most productive activity in locating new work is writing and lecturing. "We have a twice-yearly lecturing assignment at the Management Centre of Europe, talking to top executives who attend courses there. We've written a book *Planning Office Space*, which arose out of a series of articles in the AJ and we contribute quite often to magazines, both in the architectural field and also in some management journals." Various senior partners speak regularly at conferences and this often brings in work from delegates. DEGW also run informal in-house seminars to which they invite other architects. They too are a source of work, since architects use DEGW as sub-consultants on space planning problems. For instance, DEGW supported Ahrends, Burton and Koralek at the early stages of the Cummins Diesel project at Shotts in Scotland. A further source, for keeping in touch with contacts, is a new magazine called *Facilities* which they have started as a joint venture with the Architectural Press and which deals with the new discipline of buildings management.

Contacts are, of course, what most often arises in the first instance from these various ventures, and these are fed into DEGW's internal promotion group which divides prospects into "leads, possibles and probables". An annotated list is produced on a word processor and circulates around the office.

The fact that so many of DEGW's activities cannot be immediately validated in terms of jobs means that a considerable degree of discipline has to be imposed in keeping time sheets and records. "Everybody keeps time sheets", John Worthington says. "They're divided into above and below the line activities. Above the line ones are those with fees attached—when you're directly engaged on a job. Below the line is the gamut of activities which we call 'practice development and promotion'. These can involve anything from spending an evening chatting with a possible client to looking at a site on which we're considering making a proposal to a developer."

More generally, though, their course of action is to respond to a request to make a proposal for a particular scheme. DEGW's proposals seem to be different from those of many practices inasmuch as they are primarily in written rather than graphic form. "We spend at least a couple of days on even a minor proposal", Worthington says. "From an internal point of view an important part of that exercise is estimating how much time the job will take, because if it's a consultancy assignment, as is often the case, we quote a lump sum. We do however leave ourselves some leeway for further negotiation if the job runs over the time estimate. One seldom gets a specification so exact that you can measure the time element with absolute accuracy."

An outline proposal like that would normally be made without charge, but beyond that DEGW do very little work for nothing. In rare instances, Worthington says, they might hesitate to press their fee for a known client where a building decision depended on planning permission, but on the whole, "it's a great mistake for clients as well as architects to do feasibility studies for nothing—though I suspect some people do it. For one thing they are valuable in their own right and involve a lot of work..."

The architect is less likely to give impartial advice if his fee depends on the building going ahead. There are times when one's advice to clients should be not to build.

The nature of DEGW's work means that they have tended to drift away from what is generally regarded as orthodox architectural work into more of a consultancy role, producing concepts and designs directly related to their studies of building use and organisational structure. Worthington makes no apologies for this. "Architects have to be flexible in a market that is changing all the time now. That's much more difficult if you have, say, a large production office to keep occupied or a mainframe computer that has to be fed with work. We've been able to move into new fields like science parks because we're flexible—as well as to keep up with changes in our own backyard."

Part of that policy of flexibility has been DEGW's Mexican venture and it has, in part, been a cautionary tale. "It's taken a lot more of our energies than we anticipated and because of the economic situation in Mexico it hasn't made the contribution we anticipated. On the other hand we believe that the fact that we've made a real and visible commitment to the country will pay off in the end. We've also got some multi-national clients through it, in a roundabout way."

The ultimate test of flexibility, though, is the long-term future of the practice. There is a tendency for firms to fall apart after a while or at least to lose their initial impetus. Here Frank Duffy has some interesting views, based on his study of the nature of organisations. "A practice should keep renewing itself by continuing to learn and continuing to bring in new blood, rather like an Oxford college. There should also be a central objective which should always be kept in mind, even if it's adapted from time to time. It's in the light of that that practice decisions should be made."

Elsom Pack & Roberts

At one time a client used to approach you and you knew that he wanted you for that job. Nowadays you're one of four or five firms he'll speak to, and he wants to look round your office, look at the structure of the partnership, your finances and even the extent of the insurance you carry.

The changing conditions of practice are a matter more of regret than concern to Cecil Elsom, senior partner in what has been one of the most consistently successful practices over the entire post-war period. Most of their work is in office buildings within a contract range of £3m–£30m and almost all of it is in the UK. In their time they have designed most building types except hospitals. "I don't like jobs that run on for a great length of time", Elsom says. "We like to be in and out within three years, though these days getting planning consents tends to delay things." Part of that delay involves doing preliminary work before consent to build is granted, but Elsom Pack do not do design work for nothing in the hope that the client will give them the job. "The furthest we'd stretch the point is to work for cost for a while for an established client, but frankly we've seldom been in that position. Because of our position as highly successful developers' architects we tend to get highly professional and competent clients who normally already have a site with planning permission." Because of their record, Elsom Pack also gets approaches from less established developers. In that case they do some discreet checking at Companies House and around their contacts to make sure they don't get involved in fruitless work.

One reason why Elsom Pack's position is secure is that they

The Architects

have managed to combine high design standards with their acknowledged expertise in meeting commercial criteria—for instance, their scheme around Westminster Cathedral is one of the happier examples of shop and office development to be seen in London. The secret, Elsom says, is to have a clear image of what your practice is trying to achieve and to stick to it. His watchword is all-round competence, and he thinks a practice can ultimately achieve more that way than by having a high profile as designers. "There are certain dangers in being a high profile practice. You tend to attract the attention of planning committees who are often politically motivated in their actions. I think we get what we want for our clients oftener than some of our competitors. We rely on competence to get things done."

That also applies to marketing. "We never approach a client, and the relaxation of the Code has made no difference to what we do. We do a certain amount of wining and dining and encourage the younger partners to do so as well, but that's all." Nevertheless, he is very much aware that times are changing, as his opening quote shows. He says that a new twist is the interest shown indirectly by the banks in the financial status of architects involved in major development projects. When they advance large sums to a client they want to be sure that the architect will not let him down and has the resources to handle the job.

Unlike some fairly similar practices, Elsom Pack have never looked for work abroad. "We considered it during the recession, but fortunately jobs came along at the right time. I'm glad that happened now."

I'm not a great believer in having offices all over the place—you can't control things that way. All we have is a small, two-roomed offshoot in Edinburgh.

Elsom Packs's main office in London employs a staff of about a hundred, though he began after the war with a £1200 job for one client. That client happened to be Max Rayne, now Lord Rayne and chairman of London Merchant Securities. He thinks a lot of successful practices begin by finding one good client, though ultimately there is a danger of becoming too closely identified with him if you don't branch out. "I realised that when somebody asked me many years ago why I didn't start my own practice—he thought I was employed by Max."

Fitzroy Robinson Partnership

The big problem with a firm like ours is that our clients get old along with us. That may be why so few architectural practices last more than a couple of generations—people split off and take their contacts with them. You've got to be careful to bring along new talent and get them to work with their opposite numbers in client organisations.

It is not surprising to find Fitzroy Robinson partner J. G. McLeish emphasising the importance of contacts because it is generally thought that its founder's City network played a large part in making the practice one of the most successful firms over the last 30 years. Started in 1956, they have a staff of 250, making them one of the largest practices in Europe. Their clients include most of the big property companies, pensions funds and banks in the UK.

To some extent such work creates its own momentum. "One job leads to another", says McLeish. "For instance Trafalgar House were the developers for the London office of the Bank of Commerce and Credit and that led to our doing banks for that same Arab client in Dubai and Abu Dhabi."

But he feels that things have got a great deal tougher. "At one time you'd just get the client's instructions and come up with a solution. Now the important thing is to be able to satisfy the planners. You have to be able to provide answers about density, servicing, traffic, illumination and external materials as well as the appearance of the building." Clients too are aware that they are in a buyer's market. Every presentation, McLeish says, is a competition. "You're always aware that the client is looking at more than one proposal." Furthermore that competition is not only from other architects. There is an increasing pressure from project managers who, he says, get the same fee as architects but are not subject to the same amount of liability. He thinks this is wrong. "Very few liabilities claims occur through design failure. They're mostly due to things that have occurred in the building process. If architects are going to be working for a lower fee for just doing the design work, they should also have a lower liability for indemnity claims."

Architects, he thinks, are going to have to fight much harder for their share of the cake in a number of ways, but Fitzroy Robinson are still studying what moves they should make in the light of changes in the Code. At any rate they do not believe that courting the media will play a large part in their plans. "We've never been the favourites of the AJ or the AR—the papers on the left of the architectural spectrum whose gods have been the Fosters, the Farrells and Stirlings. That fact has not stopped us getting work, though." Nor have they found PR much of a help. They did try using a PR firm once, but felt that they did not understand the process of architecture. "I think a lot of marketing ideas work in the USA that don't work here, because they have now had ten years to develop marketing strategies that are relevant to the profession." On the other hand McLeish believes that the changes in the Code will leave Fitzroy Robinson almost infinite scope for any policies that they do decide to formulate. "Since nothing appears to be forbidden, it follows that anything is permitted."

GMW Partnership

It is not just a question of cultivating clients by joining clubs, though inevitably our partners run across people who may be potential clients in the course of their social life or leisure activities. One of the ways to obtain clients is through a community of interests. It is as good an indicator to the all-important matter of personal chemistry as any other.

With a staff of 150 including 13 partners and 13 associates, GMW have built up a network of contacts since the practice began as Gollins Melvin & Ward, originally founded in 1947. They are one of the heavyweights among British practices, with offices on the Continent and in the Middle East as well as a large London headquarters. Much of their work has been on prestige projects: offices for large companies, universities, hospitals, schools and airports. They read almost like a roll call of major buildings in the private and public sector in the past two decades: the new Covent Garden Market building, the central redevelopment of the University of Sheffield, the BA terminal at JFK in New York, the European Headquarters of American Express at Brighton. Housing plays a comparatively minor role in their range at present.

In spite of their size, GMW are not a multi-disciplinary practice, but partner Tony Gregson says this very circumstance can itself be a source of work. It often comes in through recommendations from other building professionals who pass their name on to clients or who bring them into schemes they themselves are working on. A case in point is the design of the new Mombasa Airport which came through a recommendation from the engineers Scott Wilson Kirkpatrick, with whom they have often worked before.

Airports are one area in which GMW have developed special expertise and the way they keep up with news in that building type is typical of their approach overall. "We read as many specialist magazines as possible, such as *Flight, Aviation Week, Airport Forum, Airport International*, in the airport field. We also keep up on the technical press and the generalist financial press, including the *Financial Times* and the *Economist*. We also subscribe to a government publication, *Export Intelligence Services*, which we have found quite useful in giving us advance news of overseas projects."

GMW have obtained work through the Clients' Advisory Service of the RIBA and they do actively market their product where possible. They regard marketing as essential for small up-and-coming practices as well as for established ones. They did have a tentative flirtation with a PR consultancy but are managing without one at present. They also have a range of in-house resources for presenting their work. For instance they have their own interior design department, graphic studio, printing and model-making facilities. These activities are reflected in their professionally produced practice brochure. It is more like a book and illustrates the whole range of their work, largely in colour, with brief texts and plans as well as photographs. It is divided into various building types, so that individual modules can be broken out and sent to clients as required. The graphic design side has recently been employed putting together an exhibit of GMW's work for an international conservation conference in Basel and subsequently repeated in London, and are participating in an expo at the RIBA during January and February this year. There has been a lot of interest, but no tangible results as yet.

Entering competitions does play a part in GMW's marketing strategy and they have been successful in a number of them, but they think one should not lay too much emphasis on competitions as a means of getting work, though they are becoming more prevalent after a long fallow period. "They are extremely time-consuming and expensive to go in for. Traditionally open competitions were analysed by considering the sponsors and the assessors and their likelihood to be favourably disposed towards the kind of solution you are offering. They can be a way of doing a lot of work and not being paid for it."

A firm of GMW's size and carrying the overheads they do must keep the clock running most of the time. For that reason, they tend to charge clients on a time basis for speculative work and merge the fee after, say, planning consent has been obtained and the job goes ahead.

Some practices have diversified by expanding their activities outside the purely architectural field. GMW are a notable case in point, with their involvement in interior design and computers. GMW Computers Ltd is now a separate company, but it began ten years ago when GMW considered they should investigate the opportunities of CAD more closely. They appointed a full-time consultant for two years, giving him a very clear specification of what the firm wanted to achieve. It was a well-timed move and GMW Computers now provides its services and programs to many other practices apart from its own. However, getting into computers is not a soft option and can be expensive when elaborate equipment is involved. CAD provides a valuable service to the practice but it is difficult to identify exactly how it contributes directly to costs, although GMW know it contributes directly to efficiency.

In spite of the consultancy-like nature of GMW's activities in this and in most specialist building areas, GMW profoundly disagree with those who see a diminishing role for many of the things an architectural practice traditionally does.

All partners and staff have special interests and areas of expertise and we think that the future of architects will incorporate concepts of services including interior design, project management and computer-aided design as part of the service, should they be required by the client for that particular commission.

Holder and Mathias Partnership

The transfer of a job from a senior partner to another member of the practice has to be handled circumspectly. The client mustn't be left with the feeling that he's being fobbed off with somebody more junior once he's committed himself to us. It's a question of persuading him that we're genuinely a team. I'm the captain, but any member is capable of scoring tries.

Peter Mathias regards making the initial client contact and then gradually meshing it into the work of the practice as an important aspect of his and Tim Holder's role. It is natural, perhaps, that he should use a rugby metaphor because although a large part of the Holder and Mathias Partnership's work is now around London, the roots and origins of their practice are in Wales. It was founded in 1968 and has offices in Swansea and Cardiff. Its 100 employees mean that it has grown fairly rapidly—a problem they have tackled by running the practice as ten operating groups, each headed by a partner or associate. The average contract value of their work is around £1.5m and it is centred on industrial, commercial and health and welfare buildings. Planning consultancy is also an important part of it.

Surprisingly for a practice that, though well-established, is not a household name, their spacious London office is in the heart of Mayfair—one of the world's more expensive locations. It puts them geographically close to the offices of some of their bigger clients, as well as to prestige business hotels like the Connaught and the Hilton. The choice of that location is part of the way Peter Mathias sees the practice. "It wouldn't be appropriate for us to be in a converted workspace in Paddington", he says. "We don't claim to be in the vanguard of the profession in matters of design. We do however maintain a high standard of quality, coupled with efficiency and economy in getting the job done."

Though a lot of their work is in Wales and all the partners are either Welsh or Welsh-trained, Mathias feels that it is competence rather than favoured treatment for a locally based practice that has been responsible for their progress. The strength of the Welsh Mafia (the cultural establishment) or the Taffia (locally elected officials and their chums) is not what it was, though involvement in local causes and activities continues to be a plus point. He himself, for instance, was chairman of the RIBA branch in Cardiff and Vice-President of the Society of Architects in Wales, and he thinks this could have helped when the name of the practice was put forward by the Clients' Advisory Service to local enquirers. However, in the main he regards the benefits of such activities as indirect and at least partly a question of "putting something back in the profession" like his current membership of the RIBA Council. That takes up at least one day a week and means that effectively he has to work a seven-day week. He doesn't mind that, though he says that ultimately you have to balance committee work against the demands of the practice. "It's easy to get co-opted into all sorts of activities to the detriment of your main job. You have to say no sometimes."

In part Mathias sees his RIBA activities as helping to foster the image of the practice and he and his fellow managing partner spend about 50 per cent of their time doing things which are directly or indirectly concerned with getting work. "The direct part consists mainly of finding sites and matching clients to them. We also have a technical manager in the practice who does this full-time. He's a young ex-local authority project manager with excellent contacts who's also good at dealing with people." For a growing practice, though, he feels that selecting clients is as important as finding them. "You have to have a concept of the directions in which you want to develop. It may be that you want to concentrate in certain spheres, or you may simply want bigger and more secure clients; or both. As your practice gets bigger you tend to find that jobs under a certain contract value become uneconomic.

In their case he feels that the threshold is under £50,000, but they would not turn a job away simply because it was too small.

If a job is too small for us we would try to refer the client to a smaller but competent practice. Quite a few larger firms have the problem of being offered jobs that are sub-economic in their terms, but which would be profitable for a new practice with smaller overheads. I would say that anyone starting up ought to keep on good terms and in regular contact with larger practices in his area.

Some of these jobs are handed over to employees who also do outside work—a permitted form of moonlighting. Mathias feels that this can be a rewarding form of training—in every sense of the word—and he says that he and Tim Holder cut their own architectural teeth doing small jobs like home extensions. But there are obvious perils that need to be controlled. "It's very hard to draw the borderline between practice time and resources and your own work—even more so because doing your first private job is enormously exciting. It can easily become all-absorbing, to the detriment of the employer's practice."

Holder and Mathias's clients are mainly large institutional and commercial ones, and here they stress the range of expertise they can make available. "Planning consultancy is particularly important these days and in provincial and rural areas may depend on a good deal of local knowledge. The role of conservation committees has increased considerably in recent years and there are often conflicts to be resolved between what we think are the best technical or design solutions and, say, conditions laid down over the use of local materials by a conservation lobby." The need for all sorts of bits of specialised expertise means that Mathias sees the role of architects like himself to be moving increasingly into orchestrating teams of specialists, either in-house or co-opted. "Design management and direct professional control is I think where the future of the profession lies, rather than in becoming developers."

The skills of the practice are summarised in a brochure which sets out their main lines of work with some colour illustrations and a description of their organisation, resources and experience. This central document is backed up, as necessary, by data sheets giving more detail about specific types of work. These are left with clients after a presentation. How much money they spend on these depends on the likelihood of work arising from them. "Our basic package is a slide show about our work—not a video because you lose the personal touch if you simply run a film. However we do, on occasion, spend as much as £10,000—counting the practice's time as well as actual resources—on a really important one. That's about the same as it costs to enter an invited competition."

Mathias thinks that competitive tendering on fees will become more widespread. "We keep very accurate historical records of costs which enables us to quote competitively in the first instance. Thereafter the margin we're prepared to adjust is quite tiny—say 0.1% in a 5% quotation base. Otherwise we would feel that we would be compromising the quality of what we're offering the client and that is to no one's advantage."

On completion all their buildings are photographed, but only for record purposes by one of the staff or a local photographer. Professional architectural photography is enormously expensive and should be confined, in Mathias's opinion, to the buildings that really merit "Oscar treatment." They do, however, use an outside PR company quite regularly in conjunction with Holder and Mathias's own in-house graphics department. The key factor, he says, is to take care over the wording of press releases, and you have to be prepared to spend time over that. "You've got to get the reader's attention in the first five lines."

Ninety per cent of Holder and Mathias's work is in the UK, but Peter Mathias sees working abroad as a growth area, though the costs are enormous. For that reason they have gone into a consortium with an American firm under the name of HMTW International. This enables them in their brochure to offer clients a far wider and more imposing range of overseas work than would be represented by Holder and Mathias alone, but the advantages to their American partners, of getting access to a British firm's range of skills and contacts, are mutual. Even indirectly such a relationship can offer benefits in terms of giving both partners wider horizons, which in this case are scanned at twice-yearly board meetings, either in New York or in Wales.

Howell Killick Partridge & Amis

We've worked on the basis of never taking on more work than the partners could handle. We would turn down work if we couldn't give it full partner service. That means that each one of us should not have more than one job at the design stage, one in production drawings and one under construction at any one time.

In his book about their practice, Sherban Cantacuzino wrote of the four founding partners of Howell Killick Partridge & Amis, "All four were designers and they came together determined to keep design in their own hands." The emphasis on this kind of personal involvement meant that the sudden untimely deaths of Bill Howell and John Killick within two years of each other in 1972 and 1974 was a blow from which few similarly based firms would have recovered. It is possible, though, that the rigorous policy they had from the very start in 1959 of limiting the amount of work they took on also helped to limit the impact of this double loss. At any rate, the practice not only survived but has emerged as one of the most successful and highly regarded medium-sized partnerships around today. Indeed with a staff of only 30, they are at the smaller end of the spectrum, though they have some impressively large jobs on the drawing board: a £25m contract-value submarine base at Devonport (now completed), the £20m Hall of Justice in Trinidad (the result of winning a competition) and, most recently, a £33m new prison at Woolwich. There are also many jobs in the £250,000 plus range, many of which have won awards and commendations.

The quality of the practice's work has always been high

and John Partridge feels that this reputation has been their most effective marketing tool. His apparently casual approach is however belied by HKPA's highly professional brochure which, apart from listing an impressive number of awards, makes two statements which must appeal greatly to clients. Firstly it stresses the intense degree of partner involvement in design: "our buildings are designed personally by the partners, all of whom work on the drawing board". Secondly it places great emphasis on cost control: "the number of variations and the cost implications of unforeseen problems are monitored by the quantity surveyors and regular financial statements predicting the final cost are reported to the client."

HKPA began their career as the finalists in the competition for Churchill College, Cambridge and throughout the 'sixties and 'seventies educational buildings, particularly in the tertiary sector, were an important part of their workload. This inevitably gives a practice a somewhat establishment flavour, and it is not surprising that John Partridge has been prominent in the activities of various RIBA committees and that he is currently Chairman of the increasingly powerful body which represents the interests of many of the larger private sector practices: the Association of Consultant Architects.

He is also, as was his colleague Bill Howell before him, an ARA. The Royal Academy in recent years, and perhaps more especially under the presidency of Sir Hugh Casson, has gained new prestige as a platform for architects' work and that section attracts almost as much attention and comment now as the paintings. An increasing number of architects submit models and drawings to the Summer Show, including those who, like Norman Foster, are notoriously choosy in these matters. The reason for this is that it is felt by architects to be a highly effective way of bringing themselves to the notice of influential clients and if this is so, then to be an Academician must be doubly significant.

John Partridge himself is, of course, somewhat unforth-

The Architects

coming about this aspect. He does, however, point to the fact that HKPA are one of the very few practices to have had an exhibition of their work at the Heinz Gallery, that they have had a book written about the practice and that they have all their buildings professionally photographed. Otherwise he does not do much to publicise the practice, though he keeps in touch informally with clients.

On the other hand he is aware that going after large jobs is a highly competitive business these days and needs very careful presentation. "You're on view all the time", he says. "The process whereby we got the Woolwich Prison job spanned over two and a half years and took in interviews, presentations and being asked along by the PSA to give crits. Each one of those is an event at which you're being measured up." This requires mental flexibility and a feeling for the atmosphere of the occasion. At one presentation for the PSA for instance, he became aware that his prepared approach was the wrong tack to take, so he did it quite differently, off the cuff.

His strong, if instinctive, feeling for marketing is also manifested in his comments on getting work overseas:

Overseas clients are not usually interested in your record of doing low cost housing as evidence of design ability for tackling a range of building types. Quite the reverse. If you're trying to win a prestige job it's no use telling them about all the low cost, socially conscious work you've done elsewhere.

You also have to be aware of the fact that appearances may matter, at least in the first instance, as much as reputations—indeed that the one may be seen as validating the other. "One architect I know was trying to win a contract in Egypt and he arrived on a cheap flight at 4am. That finished him before he had even started. On such occasions a first class ticket may be a necessary investment."

At the moment HKPA have as much work as they can handle, so do they have any plans to expand and abandon their faith in staying small? "It's very difficult to stand still", John Partridge says. "But whatever we do, we wouldn't depart from our policy of offering clients the kind of team they can relate to, which we've found to be a partner plus a seven-person group."

Hulme Chadwick & Partners

A brochure sent out of the blue will only get looked at if it's as good as the Pirelli calendar.

Andrew Chadwick has strong views on graphics and his firm takes a more eclectic view of what architectural practice consists of than most. There is a historical precedent in this because his father, who started the practice in 1946, was president of SIAD and was responsible for one of the classics of post-war design—Wilkinson Sword's garden tools. Today Hulme Chadwick are still involved in industrial and exhibition design and are responsible for the corporate identity of Bass Charrington, though their most significant diversification, of which more later, has been in computer drafting.

Their architectural work is mostly concerned with rehabilitation and refurbishment, though such jobs can be very substantial with a contract value which, in their case, now ranges between £60,000 and £3m. To provide an appropriate workload for his 20-person practice, Andrew Chadwick tries to develop a pattern of one major project every couple of years, backed up with a number of minor ones. Some of his methods of getting work are conventional. "We're major users of the lunch circuit", he says. In other cases it is a question of identifying factors that may be of interest to clients and then making a direct approach with a brochure and a letter. "A well-written letter is essential—you've got to take the trouble to pick out something that will really strike a chord with the reader: identify a real need that you think he might have and put forward an intriguing but very brief case for why you think you might be able to handle it."

The brochure reinforces the argument. Hulme Chadwick's consists of a neat folder into which A4 landscaped cards illustrating various jobs can be slipped, according to what the potential client might be interested in. It is jargon free, describes what the client's problems were in each case, how Hulme Chadwick solved them, at what cost and within what period of time. The important thing, Chadwick says, is to create an air of confidence that skills already displayed in one area can be extended into another.

Some smaller or new practices complain that the Clients' Advisory Service only passes crumbs from the tables of its favourite sons on to them. Andrew Chadwick does not share that view. "You never know when a small job might turn into something much bigger or a smaller client may go on to greater things. Our biggest job, redesigning the world headquarters of a business machine company, began as a rather modest referral from CAS to rehabilitate 1500 square feet of office space in North London."

He also stresses the importance, particularly for a new practice, of taking trouble over even unlikely leads. "A while ago I got to hear about the owner of a caravan park in Great Yarmouth who was looking for an architect to design an amusement arcade. None of the locals were very keen, but I took the trouble to drive up there through the snow. The client was impressed with that and we got the job, which turned out to be quite a good one."

Taking trouble over such obvious things is, he believes, a more effective way of marketing the practice than PR. They even tried having a marketing man in house, but it didn't work. "The disciplines of marketing as they're understood in the PR world simply don't apply to architecture—it's a service not a product. It's no use sending out mass-produced handouts. You have to find a different angle for every medium and every editor."

Though he says that stories about the practice can be useful if you use them to validate and back up claims about it when talking to clients, he has found that the most useful

The Architects

form of publicity are the "events" which Hulme Chadwick run about twice a year. These are now mainly tied into their computer consultancy and they invite present and potential clients along—they keep about 2000 of their names on their computer file. Many of their clients are in fact other architects, but they don't see Hulme Chadwick as competitors in this specialised sphere. Andrew Chadwick also has an official role in it in his capacity as chairman of the RIBA Computer Group.

Chadwick thinks that architects should use events more often as a way of getting into the news:

Maybe buildings should be launched like ships. There are such things as building openings and laying foundation stones, but for some reason they don't make the news like ship launchings, even though the values are comparable.

He also thinks that in-house events should become a more regular way of spreading awareness about a practice, though you have to be able to show the people who come to them something that will really interest them. In the case of Hulme Chadwick, of course, that would be something like a hands-on exercise with some of their very sophisticated drafting machinery.

Their involvement in this sphere—they are in fact one of the acknowledged leaders in it—was a marvellous example of turning a potential disaster to good account. Three years ago they won a contract from London Transport to refurbish two major underground stations and Andrew Chadwick decided a computer was essential to meet the tight deadline. He was already committed to the purchase of £100,000 worth of equipment when the contract was cancelled. Instead of losing heart, Chadwick set up a computer drafting bureau for other architects under the name of CCD Computer Drafting. It was a well-timed move, coming as it did at just about the time that interest in these techniques as a way of handling production drawings suddenly sharpened—along with the uncomfortable awareness of the fact that most architects lacked the necessary skills in this new area of practice or even the know-how to make sensible purchasing decisions in a field where mistakes could be fearsomely expensive. Today CCD Computer Drafting offers a wide range of services from consultancy and training to producing work for other offices. To the many who believe firms must specialise to make a mark, Hulme Chadwick are a portent of the shape of practices in the future.

Levitt Bernstein Associates

We circulate news editors of the main professional and trade papers when we have a story for them. In many cases they're only too glad to get such information. They can't afford to go round the country hunting for stories, so they tend to write up the big well-known practices. They'd just as soon write up good work by lesser-known firms—but they have to get to hear about it.

These days it is probably true to say that what Levitt Bernstein Associates do already has a *prima facie* news value because they would come to most people's minds as one of the more interesting and enterprising practices to emerge since the 1970s. They first came to prominence with their much publicised and premiated Manchester Exchange Theatre, but before then they had already built up a solid base with their work for housing associations and co-operatives.

In the late 'sixties, David Bernstein was one of the first architects to spot the potential of housing associations. These are generally—though not always—non-profit making bodies who fund approved schemes with money from the government's Housing Corporation and from local authorities. With that money they buy sites, develop them, rent or sell them to tenants and then maintain them. They also advise housing co-operatives—groups of tenants who band together to buy rented properties from a landlord and upgrade them. "Housing associations have become the new wave in housing after the great public sector boom of the 'sixties", Bernstein says. "First you had the great charitable foundations like the Peabodys of the 19th century, then you had council housing and now you have housing associations". Though the Housing Corporation has suffered from government cutbacks lately, Bernstein says their approach to housing has bi-partisan support and is not likely to be reversed with a change of government. (A list of them is produced by The National Federation of Housing Associations, 30 Southampton Street, London WC2).

Though they are non-profit making they employ largeish and increasingly expert staff who keep a sharp eye open for architects with demonstrable expertise and become substantial repeat clients for those they can work happily with. Quite a lot of that work is concerned with rehabilitation and conversion and Levitt Bernstein validated their abilities in this field by writing two books about it, one on supervision and one on specification. The authorship was ascribed to the practice and though in money terms the income from them was modest in comparison to professional fees, they turned out to be tremendously good for publicity. For the same reason David Bernstein thinks that attending and speaking at conferences where potential clients are present is highly effective.

He also has pronounced views on the value of press publicity. Though there clearly is a value in being written up in the professional press, if you want to reach clients directly through the media you need to get into the ordinary newspapers and the approach in your press release has to be quite different. "The specialist magazines are obviously interested in the technical angle. For the others you have to find an aspect of the story which has a more general appeal. For instance in the press release for the housebuilding company we formed we mentioned that we were offering built-in kitchen appliances and a 'ready to move in' low-cost furnishing scheme. That brought a write-up in the *Evening Standard* and a tremendous response from buyers."

One of the uses that can be made of stories about the practice and its work in specialist magazines is to get offprints and send those to potential clients who would not normally see the magazines. Though Levitt Bernstein do not do much in the way of concerted marketing David Bernstein was much impressed by some aspects of the RIBA seminar on the subject conducted by the American expert Weld Coxe—in particular his system of classifying potential clients. Coxe divides these into "influencers" who have the ear of a smaller group of "decision makers" and who can both only be reached through what he calls "gatekeepers" (eg, the managing director's secretary) whose importance is greater than their apparent position in the client's hierarchy. Bernstein asked everybody in the practice to come up with contacts who came under these headings and the resultant trawl produced several hundred names for their mailing list.

He has also changed his views about the practice brochure, which is in the process of being revised. He now considers it was too wordy and did not have enough visual interest. "The trap is to produce a brochure which impresses other architects rather than clients", he says. Like that of many other practices, the new one will be built up as a set of modules which can be assembled as necessary, accompanied by a small master brochure which summarises their work as a whole.

Bernstein is doubtful about joining clubs as a way of making client contacts and anyway is not a joiner by nature. He has also had reservations about the Clients' Advisory Service which at least in the past he suspected of being "a bit of an old boy network", though the firm has lately received an important commission through them. Ultimately he believes the best source of work is referrals, either from clients or from fellow professionals in other branches of building. "That's why it's a good thing to move into a growing field like housing associations—one's clients tend to move up or into other associations or organisations of a different kind."

When they get to the stage of making a presentation, Levitt Bernstein go to considerable lengths—and cost—to prepare their case. They show slides, discuss the range of their work and take the client on a tour of relevant buildings. Where a specific project is under discussion they would photograph the site and show how they would tackle it. The important thing on these occasions is to concentrate on the proposed project, not on one's past history, however glorious. "The only really important feature of your track record, as far as a lot of clients are concerned, is whether your projects were completed on time and to budget." Perhaps it was for this reason that they won the commission for the Manchester Exchange Theatre although they had never done such a building before. "We had no pre-conceived notions about it. What we were prepared to offer was our willingness to work with the client to produce the building he wanted."

Levitt Bernstein are not afraid to tread new ground, and they are one of the few practices who have taken advantage of the relaxation in the RIBA Code to set up a development company: Pilot Properties Ltd.

We've always felt that developers make more of a mystique of what they do than the circumstances justify. We happened to have some spare cash, so we decided to buy a site which had been given planning permission for flats. We decided to put two-storey houses on it—20 of them, for owner occupation.

They went to a bank who lent them half the purchase price and two-thirds of the development costs on the basis of their cash-flow forecast. The lender's confidence—and their own—was amply justified. All the units were sold well ahead of the time they had allowed, for prices between £29,000 and £37,500. It gave them quite a lot of money and invaluable experience. Most important of all, Bernstein feels, is that the experiment demonstrated to housing associations who had been showing signs of going to package dealers that a firm of architects could do everything the packagers could do—and arguably come up with a higher standard of design.

Owen Luder Partnership

There was a tremendous amount of hypocrisy before the changes in the Code. The theory was that you put up your brass plate and the clients came running, though everyone knew that it didn't work that way in practice. Any kind of printed promotion was forbidden if you paid for it, so you had to get publicity, like you got clients, in various roundabout ways. I don't think it did much for the ethics of the profession.

It was under Owen Luder's presidency of the RIBA from 1981–1983 that the RIBA Code of Professional Conduct was changed—a step he had advocated as long ago as 1963, when he wrote what was then a very contentious article in the AJ saying that it was time that the formation of practices as limited liability companies, publicity and more active marketing should all be allowed. His view of change as applied to his own practice is, however, more pragmatic than revolutionary. The Owen Luder Partnership, started in 1958, now employs 30–40 people on average and has been involved mainly in commercial developments of various kinds though their biggest current jobs are a prison and a number of large buildings around the Belvoir Coal Mine. In other words Luder is a generalist architect and sees the practice in that light when it comes to marketing. "I think it's a good idea to have some specialist skills available—for instance we have special expertise as planners and it was in that role that we became involved in the Belvoir Coal Mine Scheme. We were asked to do the environmental impact study in the first instance and that led to our being asked to design the buildings. On the other hand if you specialise too much you become vulnerable when conditions change—as they have once or twice during the years I've been in practice." The other two points he considers in looking for work are his preference for fast track schemes and for a mixture of new and familiar jobs. "Otherwise," he says, "you get stale."

Beyond that, Luder does not have a concerted marketing plan, though he is keenly aware of the importance of identifying and keeping in touch with decision makers at all levels within an organisation. You also have to be able to identify who makes what decision at different stages of the job. Some of them may be made by the staff architect, others by the managing director. "It's worth poking around a bit to see who makes the ones that mostly affect you. This is doubly important because of the close relationship between architect and client when the job gets under way. You have to make sure that people who are working together on each side really get on." Like many other architects, Luder says problems tend to arise if you introduce a new architect into the job during its course—though this shouldn't happen if you employ really good and competent staff.

He says that it is increasingly common nowadays for clients to check out a practice fairly carefully before giving them a commission for the first time. "They will talk to other clients, look at your work—even get reports on you from contractors." First impressions, though, continue to be important. For that reason you have to have a good brochure. The best kind, in his view, is a loose-leaf collection of materials that can be assembled to meet particular situations and still look professional.

Getting work is also a matter of reading the kind of media that will give you some insight into the political and economic indicators, though he says it is important not to over-commit yourself in any one direction. "We got the importance of overseas work right in the 'seventies but some snags did appear as time went on. You seldom get paid all your fees and then there are the political and economic risks. We very nearly got embroiled in Iran, but I went over myself and didn't like what I saw. However, we've had a very fruitful partnership with a local architect in Saudi Arabia. Incidentally we have no written agreement with him. It's all done on trust and I suspect that this is true of a lot of such arrangements. You could never enforce a legal agreement anyway if things go sour."

One area where Luder's experience overseas has stood him in good stead is the thorny question of competing on price. On the whole he is not happy with it unless it's within very strict limits:

If a client starts haggling on fees, it would be cheaper to give him £1000 to find another architect because the hassles will cost you at least that in the end.

A more sensible allocation of practice resources than doing cut-price jobs is to take on a certain amount of speculative work in conjunction with developers. "I regard that as part of the marketing plan for the practice and we allocate money to it, though not a fixed percentage. It's partly a seat-of-the-pants feeling and partly determined by our financial and tax position at the time. For instance there may be a case for siphoning off profits into speculative work towards the end of a tax year."

It is evident from such comments that Luder keeps close financial controls which are likely to stand him in good stead when he moves into what he believes to be a promising field for practices in the 'eighties—development. "Developers up to now have consisted of teams of surveyors, lawyers and accountants. I believe that architects with their ability to see the three-dimensional aspects of a problem, will have a unique contribution to make as directors of development companies, either on their own or in conjunction with property companies."

Michael Manser Associates

Setting your practice up as limited company is a much more direct and flexible way of operating. It means that directors—who would previously have been partners—can come or go without breaking up the practice, as often happens with partnerships. It also means that profits can be shared on a more equitable basis—there's no obligation to distribute them at fixed percentages. You can also leave money in the business to build up capital and perhaps fund other activities.

Michael Manser succeeded Owen Luder as president of the RIBA and it is not surprising that he shares many of his predecessor's ideas about the future of the profession—in particular the potential of architects to become developers. It is fair to say that this prospect has been viewed with considerable caution by many practices but Manser believes it is a highly creative and exciting way to work. "It gives you much more freedom to express architectural ideas than working for a client in what is essentially a subordinate position", he says. "A developer will naturally be cautious about anything involving experiment." As to the risks, he does not believe they are any greater than those involved in the normal run of practice—only different. "The secret is that there has to be something in it for everybody—for the owner, the developer and the tenants or purchasers. Where things go wrong is if one party gets greedy. And, of course, you have to have a good site and think the whole thing through properly first."

Certainly he does not think that you have to have huge resources to start out with, and in fact Michael Manser

Associates is not above medium size. It started in 1961 and has a solid track record of industrial, institutional and private work for which they have won a good number of awards. The contract value of their jobs is now between £250,000 and £9m, though they occasionally tackle smaller values as well.

Michael Manser is married to a well-known design journalist and has done quite a lot of writing himself. This gives him good media contacts, and a fair number of his schemes have been published in both the professional and general press. He is also firmly convinced of the publicity value of awards like those offered by the Civic Trust and of sending work in to the Royal Academy Summer Exhibition. Here he echoes the words of a recent RIBA *Journal* article by Stephen Games who said that the Exhibition was "a chance to advertise. Many of the visitors are potential clients."

It is through a combination of these means that he currently brings the practice to the notice of clients. His brochure is a rather basic item about the size of a large Christmas card, with pictures of some of his buildings across a range of types and an absolute minimum of text. Compared to those of some practices it might be considered less than informative, but Manser says, "When you send out a large, unwieldy piece of publicity material it tends to get put on the shelves and forgotten about. Ours stands up on the desk like a greeting card and we got some work from it right away when we first sent it out." He is now considering an annual brochure as a sort of progress report. "We'll send it to existing clients mainly. I've never felt able to approach anybody without a good reason. Doing an annual report will provide that. You lose clients if you don't stay in touch." One effective and interesting way of doing so, however, is to provide them with annual maintenance reports on previous buildings at a modest fee.

Once contact with a client is made, the practice spends a lot of money on presentations, conscious of the fact that putting up a building is probably the most substantial single investment many of them will ever make. "We like to get the client involved in helping us to get the building right. The most keenly interested clients end up with the best buildings—and those are also the ones that are the architect's best advertisements for future work."

In comparison to that he does not regard competitions as particularly effective. "I've got a moral hang-up about all that wasted effort if you don't win", he admits. "There's also the financial factor—it costs a minimum of £6000–15,000 to go in for a competition if you look at all the costs including office time. We'll probably do one or two a year, though, just to keep our hands in."

He is also aware of the increasing tendency for architects to be asked to compete for a scheme, either openly or implicitly and he says that you have to guard against situations where you are essentially being asked to work for nothing. "We're prepared to do a limited amount of speculative work for continuing clients—look at a site, do a feasibility study, maybe talk to the planning authority in a preliminary way. But only if we have a reasonable chance of getting the job eventually, and then only within strictly laid-down parameters of how far we're prepared to take things."

Those parameters definitely exclude cutting prices to get the job, and Manser does not feel that this is either a necessary or desirable step to take:

Developers respect hard and fair dealings—and they don't thank you if things go wrong as a result of taking shortcuts. Cut-price buildings nearly always produce trouble for the architect, the client or the contractor—often for all three. It is a short-term capital gain for a long-term revenue loss.

Moxley & Frankl

The key is not singleness of purpose but simply good organisation through interaction of management, skill and labour. For Gothic architecture it is the element of organisation and management that has been lost in past interpretations.

That quotation is from Andrew Saint's highly praised recent book, *The Image of the Architect*, not from Michael Moxley, but it is certainly one that his own words would echo. "It's skill in putting buildings together that produces good architecture", he says. "If a design is easy to build and if the sequence of operations has been thought through properly, there's much more likelihood that the finished building will meet the architect's objectives."

These are also ideas that his father, Ray Moxley, would endorse, but in fact the two have not practised together. Michael Moxley started on his own in 1978, having previously worked with HKPA. Two years later he was joined by Claire Frankl who had been with the Hackney Borough Council. Today they have a busy and rapidly growing practice, with a staff of four assistants, plus a part-time secretary and a part-time bookkeeper. Their biggest project to date is a £1.5m scheme with a developer for 48 houses and flats, but they do a lot of work with contract values of between £30,000 and £100,000.

Like most new practices they started with small jobs picked up from putting the word around among acquaintances and friends. Moxley also found his old employers, HKPA, generous in passing work on to him. The problem is that the moment you start running an office, the fees from small jobs become insufficient to cover costs. "I got round that to some extent by also acting as project manager in these cases. That increases the fee to something like twenty per cent of contract value. But you have to know the skills to do it successfully. I had acted as project manager in building my own house and I'd learned about plumbing and electrics among other matters. In the course of doing so I got to know a tremendous amount about the building process."

That knowledge stood him in good stead as the practice picked up larger clients. Some of them came indirectly through professional contacts of various kinds—both Moxley and his partner, Claire Frankl, have been members of the RIBA Council—but he is less than enthusiastic about the Clients' Advisory Service. "We get our most pernickety clients through them. People who work through institutional rather than personal channels are often those who have had difficulties on the personal plane.".

The practice's most fruitful contacts have been with housing associations and developers. "Housing associations are professional clients in the sense that you're dealing with fellow professionals who know the score. We've gradually built up our relationships with them from other architects." He says there is no particular way you can push the process along. "You just get a phone call, more or less out of the blue. The vital thing is to respond quickly and alertly when it happens."

With developers, however, you have to take more positive initiatives. "We read the *Estates Gazette* from cover to cover for news of sites on the market; also the property columns of the *Times, Guardian, Evening Standard* and so forth. When we see a suitable site—at the moment we're interested in residential developments in and around London—we go and look at it, do a sketch scheme and go to a developer with it. If he likes it, he files for planning permission with the local authority." That application is in the architect's name as agents for the client, so the practice then has to field numerous enquiries from contractors who are also on the look-out for developments that are under considerations. Administratively such enquiries can be something of a burden, but on the positive side it also puts the practice's name about as architects actively engaged in this type of work—and that in turn leads to their being approached by estate agents and builders with sites to sell.

Don't be shy about approaching developers, even the large ones. If you come up with a good scheme—one where the developer can see the scope for making an acceptable bid that will also give him an acceptable margin for profit—he is virtually certain to respond.

The mutuality of interests between the architect and the developer can also help with publicity. Moxley says that the developer helped to fund the publicity campaign on the Islington scheme which has been their largest job so far. But the extensive press coverage for that was not only due to the money they spent on PR. "You've got to have some kind of angle to a story if you want to get the press interested. In our case there were two. On the design side there was the fact that it was topped out with a clock tower—an unusual feature these days. The interesting technical and economical aspect was the speed with which the scheme was built. It only took eighteen months from acquiring the site to selling the last house."

Michael Moxley feels that working with developers could form a sizeable part of his practice's work-load. But whichever way the market moves, it is likely that a firm which seems to have succeeded in finding its feet between 1978 and 1983—hardly the most auspicious years for starting a practice—will have no difficulty in adjusting to the circumstances.

Moxley Jenner & Partners

For architects to concentrate on scheme design and leave project management and the general running of the job to specialists is an absolute abdication of responsibility. Involvement in the making of the building is an essential part of the architect's artistic input and it doesn't stop until the last tradesman has left the site—even the height of a door handle is important.

Moxley Jenner's approach to getting work is strongly determined by Ray Moxley's view of the service an architect ought to be offering his client. The Bristol-based practice, which came together in 1965 in a merger between his own firm and that of Michael Jenner, is multi-professional—it includes a QS partner, a landscape architect and specialists in ergonomics and planning. Unusually—but in keeping with Moxley's views—they also employ a project manager. He believes that technological advance, as well as ideology, is on their side in organising their practice around a spread of skills centering on the role of the architect. The micro means that many of the peripheral disciplines that grew up outside, such as quantity surveying, can now be controlled through the computer.

Their wide range of in-house skills is also stressed in the partnership's unusually bulky brochure. As well as illustrating an impressive amount of award-winning work spread between their three offices in Bristol, Cardiff and London and over most building types, it also makes the point that they are able to control the whole building process. Ray Moxley is a strong protagonist of AMM (Alternative Methods of Management) and an article on this subject in the brochure explains to clients what it is. Under AMM the architect controls the sub-contractors and deals with them directly. He can also sack them, which is something he can't do when there is a main contractor. Though the architect's fee is larger under AMM—which also means that he can widen the spread of profitable work—the client is still about 6 per cent better off and the job tends to get completed much more quickly. The problem is that AMM cannot be operated under the JCT 80 Form of Contract, of which Moxley is very critical. "It gives the architect very little power over the contractor, but still leaves him with all the liability." He is one of the authors of the increasingly popular ACA Contract, which redresses the balance in favour of the architect.

Moxley is an extremely active member of the ACA (Association of Consultant Architects) and was its chairman from 1974–77. That is one of a long list of offices he has held. He has been a vice-president of the RIBA, a governor of Bristol Polytechnic and chairman of DOE Housing Awards for the London region. He has also exhibited his highly accomplished drawings at the Royal West of England Academy, is a keen sailor, an amateur musician and has appeared on radio and TV. The latter are not primarily work-getting activities but he believes that having a high profile in the community and having a wide network of contacts does help on occasion. There has, for instance, been no direct spin-off from his partner Mike Jenner's regular TV appearances, but he is sure it has had an indirect result. "When a committee selects an architect the choice falls on the first one three people have heard of", he offers by way of a rule of thumb for such occasions. "Everyone in Bristol has heard of Mike Jenner, so we only have to get our name to those who don't live in that area."

Moxley is dubious about using a PR agent in facilitating that process though he does believe in keeping touch with the media. He also thinks it is extremely important to maintain contact with such sources of work as local authorities and estate agents:

Every architectural practice's workload consists of about two-thirds work from long-standing clients and one-third new work. You neglect looking for new work at your peril—there's a particular danger, when you get one or two very big clients, to do very little else. Some famous practices have gone to the wall that way.

He says estate agents are particularly important because they often hear about sites and development opportunities before they come on the market. Clients also ask them for advice about architects. On the other hand he has no ambitions at present to go into development work himself. "It's a specialised skill—I don't believe architects have the training to assess the many unfamiliar risks it involves." He also believes that the bureaucratic controls to be surmounted these days are colossal and because so many schemes fall through, the overall profits from the successful ones are not that impressive any more.

Another field where, in his view, prospects are no longer what they were is in housing association work. Cutbacks have in any case reduced the scale of the work largely to rehabs, but Moxley has found housing associations to be demanding clients and—again because of bureaucratic restrictions—slowish payers.

With some reservations he takes a rosier view of competitions, for which the practice enters with reasonable regularity. "I doubt if the costs, even for an invited comp where you're paid a fee for taking part, can be justified in direct terms, unless of course you win. But the spin-off can be valuable. Being placed second in the competition for the Abu Dhabi Conference Centre led to our being asked to design a hotel in Mombasa; and likewise our Surrey Docks entry led directly to the biggest job we have in London at the moment—the Technopark for the Prudential and the Polytechnic of the South Bank."

The practice also has work on the drawing board in places as far apart as Katmandu and Kenya, but he says you have to be careful about the financial aspect of working abroad. "I wouldn't take on work in a good many overseas countries unless payment methods were agreed beforehand", he says. "Too many people have got their fingers burnt. One has to insist on being paid in the UK in sterling." Aware of the reluctance of established architects to take on overseas jobs for that reason, a new breed of entrepreneur is appearing to facilitate payment problems. Many of them are surveyor financiers who have seen the considerable possibilities of financing major third-world building projects with international bank or Arab money.

Such jobs tend to be competitive in price terms, though Moxley says that it is fatal to cut into margins necessary to maintain the practice. However he believes that fruitful negotiations can be conducted on cutting services, some of which may not be essential. The important thing is to have a clear idea of what the priorities are, and to that end he has written a book based on his own wide-ranging experience which will give architects a clear overview of the factors to take into account (*An Architect's Guide to Fee Negotiations*, Architecture and Building Practice Guides).

In view of the spread of his interests and expertise, it is not surprising that Moxley is often called upon for his opinion and advice on architectural matters not directly connected with the practice. The most important of these he considers to be adjudication—a way of settling disputes between building professionals and contractors which is binding on signatories of the ACA Contract. It traces back, like many of the other themes in his work, to his central belief in the wide-ranging role of the architect, a role which also gives unity to an apparent diversity of activities.

MWT Architects

Direct approaches to the property divisions of potential clients, where you ask to go on the shortlist of practices being considered for a particular job can be successful, in a modest way—say about one time in twenty. But you have to do your homework carefully first—analyse what the client's problems might be. You also have to present a convincing set of credentials—in our case the track record and experience of the partners.

John Taylor is a senior partner in a practice which has gone further than many in adopting an active and coherent marketing policy. He has has been a speaker at the Weld Coxe seminars on the subject held at the RIBA, though he does not subscribe to all their ideas. Many of them, he feels are either not applicable to the UK or not acceptable to the British professional environment—for instance he does not think you can adopt "cold canvassing" approaches successfully unless you can demonstrate relevant experience. On the other hand, he is a firm believer in keeping track of job leads and following them up.

In the case of MWT this can be done centrally or locally through one of their seven UK offices. The practice was founded in 1967 by the amalgamation of two firms and now employs a staff of 102. The spread of their offices—from Truro in the west to Ipswich in the east and from Bedford on the edge of the Midlands to Southampton in the south—gives them an unusually wide range of contacts; all the more so because of the diversity of their work, which ranges through all major building types and to services such as interior and graphic design, surveying, planning consultancy and the preparation of contract documents for package-deal tenders. In spite of the growing importance of private sector clients,

111

Taylor says that one should not lose sight of the public sector. They are still responsible for allocating an enormous lot of work and each of MWT's offices register and keep in touch with all the relevant official bodies in their neighbourhood—local authorities, departments of the PSA, housing associations, hospital boards, health authorities and chief architects.

A major instrument in this process is their newsletter: MWT *Extra Dimension*. It is a simple 4-page A4 production which highlights the work of the various offices ("Hectic Workload at the Ipswich Office"), the achievements of individual partners ("Exeter's Peter Lacey joins the RIBA Establishment") and a certain amount of light-hearted staff news and general chat ("Dashing Adrian Irish from the Truro office has recently landed a modelling job.") The object of the newsletter is to provide and encourage the exchange of news between MWT's offices as well as to keep clients in the picture. They regard it as important enough to employ a professional PR man to write it. He also handles other aspects of the practice's publicity. "He collects reports of work in progress from our various offices and feeds news about it to the local—and sometimes national—press. He writes our quarterly newsletter and looks after sending out an addendum to our brochure about three or four times a year to all the people on our mailing list." John Taylor was worried at first about their PR man's style—he thought that he talked too much in lay language. They have found, though, that clients greatly prefer this to professional jargon which is sometimes only intelligible to other architects.

Another way of keeping the name of the practice in front of clients is through being active in local architectural and community causes. "There's no evidence that it produces work, but it gets written up in the papers and that's always a help." It can lead, for instance, to referrals from CAS being taken up, but Taylor thinks in the past that has tended to be conducted on a jobs for the boys basis. "The kind of central register of skills and achievements they're now setting up is a much better system."

MWT spend about £50,000 a year on promotion and presentation, but they are sparing in the amounts devoted to having their buildings photographed. "We get the job architect to take a few pictures and we only get a professional along after that if we think it's worthwhile. A good professional photographer will charge about £200–£300 a day and that's a lot of money unless we really can use the end result for promotional purposes."

A large part of their promotional effort is a matter of keeping in touch with the 70 per cent of the people on their mailing list who provide them with regular work. As far as getting new jobs is concerned, Taylor says that the most important factor is to have a thorough knowledge of the real estate market. "These days it's more a question of redevelopment and refurbishment than of greenfield sites. You've got to keep in touch with estate agents, but it's also important to keep everybody in the practice looking for opportunities—and that includes something as obvious as keeping your eyes open when you're driving along the road." Taylor cites a job they got converting a 600,000 square-foot carriage and wagon works in south Hampshire to new industrial uses simply as a result of someone driving past the site happening to notice that British Rail had put it up for sale.

John Taylor finds that another way of getting new clients is through entering competitions. "We generally come second", he says, and his implication is that this is no bad place to be—perhaps because some clients feel safer with architects in that position on design and possible cost grounds. Competing on fees, in fact, is something that he feels will become increasingly common and that it may be only a matter of time before it is introduced into work with clients like the PSA.* "It's going to demand very careful logging of practice costs." MWT are already on that track because an unusally high 20 per cent of their 102 staff are administrators, including an office manager who is an FCA. It

* This has actually happened since the interview was conducted

113

will be interesting to see what they do about advertising. At the moment they have no idea how they will approach it, but, says Taylor, now that the Code has been changed they will certainly look seriously at how the relaxation can be fitted into their marketing strategy.

A. N. Other Partnership

One of the big problems about making submissions in developing countries is to work out the scheme in enough detail to be convincing, without giving the client a blueprint for work he can take down the road to a local hack.

The A. N. Other Partnership did not want their name to be used in this book, partly because of the delicate nature of their overseas work and the frankness of their comments on it. They are a medium-sized practice with a long history of involvement in schemes abroad, including some very large ones in the Middle East and Africa. Indeed they used to run an office in the Middle East, but found it was not cost effective. "We had to include a local partner who was a bit of a passenger and we found that being on the spot didn't produce much in the way of work. That mainly came through engineering firms for whom we worked as sub-consultants."

They also came across local people who came in for scheme designs which they took elsewhere after A. N. Other had done a lot of work on them. "The ethos of copying is simply different in those countries, and of course there is no legal redress at all." As an example of how they now deal with the problem, Other explains, "We were asked to submit a design for a group of houses in a developing country. We went out for a week taking drawing boards and the material for a model with us. We went over the site, produced a complete set of preliminary drawings and prepared our model. We used that in the presentation but we left the client with only the model and a simple set of diagrams—no elevations or sections that somebody else could have worked from." According to Other, there are no hard feelings about this, or about applying pressure to get paid—another occasional hazard in working abroad. "When one of our biggest and oldest private clients got very behind with his payments we telexed him to say that we would not release further drawings until he did pay. There was a certain amount of token indignation, but it was all forgotten next time we met."

Their peripapetic style of getting work abroad is costly in terms of travel, but Other says you have to be careful about making false economies in that respect. "It's a mistake to adopt a very low and modest profile in your style of living. At any rate it should be appropriate to the client. If you're after a multi-million pound hotel complex, travelling on a cheap flight and staying in cheap hotels yourself creates a bad impression." He also thinks that being prepared to work at a reduced fee does nothing to enhance your status—quite the reverse.

Being pressured into doing an increasing amount of preliminary work on a sub-economic basis is a practice that is also creeping into the UK, and A. N. Other's own attitudes to it are interestingly ambivalent. He sits on the board of governors of a school and acted as their adviser when they were choosing an architect for an extension. "We did it on the basis of a competitive interview. First of all we asked a number of firms to submit examples of their work and to come in for a talk with the governors. We whittled down to a shortlist of three who were asked to visit the site and then be interviewed for their ideas on how they would tackle the job." They were not paid for any of that work and Other thought that was fair, though there did seem to be a large grey area of arbitrariness between that and his further comments. "When it becomes unfair is when the architect is asked to produce conceptual ideas speculatively. If you're doing that you're being asked to give away a substantial part of your expertise."

He thought, though, that this was just what you were being asked to do in planning applications. "When the planner asks you to put forward your ideas on massing and layout, he's really asking you to go beyond what you should do without a fee." Other admitted there was some discrepancy between his attitudes as an architect and as a client. In his opinion the architect in a competitive interview should ask how many submissions are being made and what the manner of selection would be. It was a matter for personal judgement if one chose to go ahead on the basis of that information.

An increasing amount of the partnership's work is now coming through UK developers who bring along their own project managers. A. N. Other have had no difficulties about operating in that way—on the contrary, they have found that when dealing with a multi-departmental client organisation the lines of communications are much clearer. So is the definition of the brief. They have found poor briefing to be the prime cause on the few occasions where things have gone wrong. "If the brief is not clear in the first instance, you should think twice about taking the job on", he says. "Knowing what work to turn down is also important."

Cedric Price

The moment you have partners and start building up staff you have to take work on to pay the bills. That's not where I want my motivation to come from.

In relation to the size of his practice, Cedric Price and his work must attract more publicity than any other architect. In fact he seems to be largely—and unapologetically—a one-man band, though he has had as many as ten people working in his office at times. However, he has never had partners and is determined that he doesn't want them. "It's a decision one has to make early on in one's professional career", he says. "If you have clear ideas about the sort of work you want to take on and how you want to run the practice, you may be better off on your own—certainly if you want to avoid run-of-the-mill hack work."

How exactly Price does get work he was reluctant to disclose. "I'm not about to give information away to my competitors", he says, citing as his reason the attempts some of them have made to supplant him, though not in ways that would have been easy to prove at an RIBA hearing. As a fairly prominent practice, one might have thought that one source of jobs would have been the Clients' Advisory Service, but Price is decidedly uncomplimentary about them. In fact he has had his name taken off their register. "They provide a very coarse match between clients and architects—for instance they suggested me to someone who wanted a design for an antique shop because I'd done work for museums. Apart from that, the register is just a historical record of what you've done, not an indication of what you'd like to do."

Doing things he likes is the cornerstone of Cedric Price's attitude to design and the principle on which he runs his practice. "I always have one scheme on the drawing board which may never get built", he says. Very often it doesn't, but as Steve Mullin showed in an interesting article in AD in 1976 this is part of a game plan which is by no means as ingenuous as Price sometimes makes it sound. His unbuilt schemes attract so much publicity—and he is so adept at maximising it—that work does emerge from them; not necessarily buildings, but glamorous, and it must be assumed remunerative, consultancies that frequently take him to Europe or America. At the time of this interview, for instance, he was in the process of turning his unsuccessful entry for the Parc de Villette competition in Paris (won by Bernard Tschumi, late of the AA and a Price disciple) into a computer graphics video showing how the Parc would have been made into a public attraction from the moment the bulldozers came on site.

The video is being put together on a mainframe computer owned by a pop group Price knows—presumably part of the extensive Price network described by Steve Mullin in that same AD article. (The subject of "networks" has received a good deal of attention of late, and a book was published in 1983 under that title. It showed how in Britain—and one suspects in other countries as well—various influence and decision groups were connected by ties of blood relationships, schools, regiments, clubs, sporting associations and so forth, which wove together some fairly unlikely personalities in a way that would otherwise have been inexplicable. This might be thought by those outside these magic circles to be a classic case of the principle of "it's not what you know, but who you know" in action, but in actual fact who you know can be an extremely effective way of ensuring that square pegs are fitted into square holes. Those in this network get to know and hear things about each other discreetly and in a way that never comes over in, say, a job interview.)

Perhaps intuitively, perhaps because he is reputed to be more of an establishment figure with establishment contacts than he likes to make out, the network principle plays an important part in Price's style of practice. "If Sir Hugh

Casson's Presidency of the Royal Academy tells us something about Sir Hugh's job-garnering network", Mullin says, "then surely we should know about Cedric's Life Presidency of the Hot Stuff Club." That club (whatever its function may be!) is part of an extensive Price network described by Mullin. It ranges from the ICA to the National Mouse Club and from the RIBA to the London Subterranean Survey Association, the Lightweight Enclosures Unit, the Science Policy Foundation, the London Library, the Labour Party and numerous other points, south, east, north and west. In his article, Mullin explains that "what distinguishes Cedric from the ordinary rut of job grubbers is that he uses his network of interests and organisations to do what he would probably call his 'preliminary sieve'. For Cedric is extremely selective about the jobs he takes on, but the selection is done by proxy, which is a canny way of saving time . . . Further advantages of this procedure are that both client and architect are likely to have a reasonable respect for each other; are each convinced that the other's interest is serious and are more likely to share a hard-headed estimate of the cost, and therefore value, of the work involved."

Mullin goes on to say that much of Price's work is "above the RIBA fee scale"—a point which Price himself confirms. Rumour has it that he has some very rich and influential private clients who are not much spoken about and about whom he himself certainly will not be persuaded to talk. If they exist, they are probably part of the circle that Mullin describes as "this great parade of politicians from left and right, industrialists, trade union officials . . . and architects of every shape and description who could never form a homogenous whole. They are there because Cedric finds them useful, or interesting or both—and vice versa."

Clearly those aspects of Price's work which attract a certain amount of derision in some architectural quarters— his highly publicised, but unbuilt schemes—are much more productive than his detractors think, or would like to think. Mullin's version is that "One can trace a whole line of related work—starting with the Thinkbelt project of 1965–6—which has led Cedric overseas, by invitation, to extend his initial published thinking in new areas . . . Interested parties pick up the argument and propose new testing grounds, at their expense."

In view of this, it is not surprising that Price's office procedures as described by Mullin are much more organised than the popular notion of a visionary architect at work. "The precise meticulous drawings that arrive on his assistant's desks each morning are incredibly compressed parcels of information which rely on a thorough two-way shorthand system operating throughout the office."

Nevertheless there does remain an enigma in the way Price has, according to Mullin, carried on "(more or less) serenely when other members of the profession have been diving through top floor windows." Whatever it is, he seems to have found a formula for successfully doing what he wants to do; to be running "an office of the right size to give him maximum involvement in its work, along with maximum extension into external fields of interest."

Richard Rogers & Partners Ltd

When we were interviewed for the Lloyds of London competition we were asked whether our design would be "another Beaubourg". Our reply was that we solve problems—we don't repeat designs. The Pompidou Centre competition proved, among other things, that we could solve the kind of problems inherent in a major project on a sensitive site.

Richard Rogers began to practice in the early 'sixties but, in circumstances which justify the *cliché*, he rocketed to a fame which today places him among the very few British architects with a genuine world reputation by winning (with his then partner, Renzo Piano) the international competition for the Pompidou Centre in the Place Beaubourg in Paris in 1971. It is fairly rare for an open competition to be won by an architect from outside the country in which it has taken place, even if he is well-known—indeed the history of such competitions is fraught with controversial decisions in which home teams have been blatantly favoured. For a little-known practice even to be placed is unusual. But that they should win—and that in France, the country which gave chauvinism its name—was quite sensational.

Marco Goldschmied, one of Rogers' three partners, believes the composition of the jury had something to do with it and that there is a lesson in this for architects thinking of entering such prestige competitions. "You should look for an architect with an international reputation on the jury and one with a strong personality who can influence the others. If the assessors are all local establishment figures an outsider has virtually no chance at all." The fact that Jean Prouvé was on the jury must have helped the Rogers + Piano entry—he would surely have been sympathetic towards the ingenious assembly of its components—but the decisive voice was Philip Johnson's. "There's a story, apocryphal probably, that when all the entries were pinned up, Johnson came to ours and said to someone, 'That's the winner, but we mustn't tell the others yet.'"

Beaubourg was officially opened in early 1977, but it is no secret that in the mid-'seventies the practice went through a very lean patch—indeed according to a *Times* article by Deyan Sudjic (23.8.82) Rogers was even thinking of dissolving it. During that time they took on a number of what they would now regard as small jobs, with a contract value of around £1m. (Now the partnership has a fairly high threshold of what they regard as uneconomic. "We wouldn't take on a £150,000 conversion unless it was to do a favour for an existing client," says Goldschmied.) Rogers himself is on record as saying, in an interview in *Building* (6.4.79) that he got virtually no work as a result of the highly praised private houses he built with Foster in his early days in the 'sixties. However, the tremendous publicity accorded to the Beaubourg scheme did lead to an invitation to take part in the £100m Lloyds competition and when they won that in 1978, a number of very important further commissions followed: a factory in France, a laboratory and a shopping centre in the USA and a micro-chip plant in Wales.

That is quite a wide spread of work in terms of building types, but the partners see no virtue in specialisation. "It's the underlying principles that are important—how you apply them to the specific problems raised by various building types is something you learn as you go along. So we don't think specialisation is necessary—in fact it may even be a disadvantage because demands change all the time." As an example of this approach in action, Goldschmied points to their highly praised INMOS micro-chip factory in Wales. "It was a big project—the value of the engineering services alone was £5m and it has an electricity supply the equivalent of that which would serve a town of 30,000 people. We completed it in 14 months—yet we knew nothing about the immensely complex processes of micro-chip production when we started."

Part of the secret was the close relationship they established with the client in developing the brief. He was in their office for three months, during which time every aspect was mapped out in tremendous detail. It is clear that Richard Rogers, despite his glamorous and innovative reputation, does not share the view of those practices who believe the architect's job should be primarily to produce a scheme design and leave the nitty-gritty to contractors and to outside consultants. They do use outside consultants to solve specific problems—on planning matters, for instance, they work closely with a firm of chartered surveyors—but they firmly believe the architect should stay in the driving seat; and know what he's doing there. "You've got to be aware of the implications of what you're designing," says Goldschmied. "Equally, you've got to be able to weigh up the implications of what consultants do or recommend you to do."

That may involve acquiring enough expertise yourself to be able to form your own opinions about what you are being told. It is partly with that motive that the partnership is, in a modest way, launching out as developers. They have acquired a two-acre site on the Thames on which to build a new office for themselves. It will form part of a complex of design-oriented workplaces. There will also be residential accommodation, and the total cost will be £3m–£4m. Putting the scheme together and raising the funds has been very instructive. "It's helped us to see some of the developer's problems—for instance the power of the financial institutions to dictate design solutions." In their case, they were forced to abandon a design incorporating a flat roof and replace it with a pitched one—apparently flat roofs are box office poison from a funding point of view.

Do they see doing their own development as a major source of work in the future? "There are architects who say that in becoming developers you run the risk of competing with your own clients, but I don't think that's the case unless you're proposing to do it on a big scale. On the contrary, I think developers are more likely to welcome working with an architect who's actually got some first-hand experience of what it's all about from a financial point of view."

This new venture of theirs has had little publicity and they do not use a PR firm. Being unquestionably one of the most newsworthy practices in the country (their name is generally bracketed with James Stirling and Norman Foster in that regard), they probably feel they get all the media coverage they want, though Goldschmied says that not all of it is welcome—referring perhaps to some of the reports that have appeared about the practice's involvement in the controversial Coin Street site. "There may be a case for having someone correct the mis-statements that are made about us", he feels. What is more surprising, even for a practice as well known as this one, is that they have no procedures for keeping in touch with past clients, though they reckon that the various speaking engagements which Rogers and other partners fulfil take place in environments where past and potential clients tend to congregate anyway: conferences for developers, for instance. There remain, nevertheless, clients they would like to meet—he mentions Clive Sinclair as a case in point—but he is fatalistic about the way work comes about:

I don't believe you can manufacture opportunities. The important thing is to be available, intelligent and willing when they arise.

When that happens, these days even a firm like Richard Rogers is not immune from having to get involved in fee negotiations. Like many other architects, Goldschmied believes that such negotiations are not a matter of haggling, but of trying to sort out priorities in the brief with the client:

125

minor design adjustments can have quite a major impact on costs. "It's important to say what you *can* do for a given sum—to take a postive view, unlike some American architects who produce long lists of what they can't do."

A further aspect of the changed climate of opinion about fee negotiations is the issue of being asked to undertake speculative work. "We'll do that up to a point and we would regard it as the equivalent of going in for a competition. But two weeks' work is about the maximum we could devote to it." On the other hand he says it is essential to do such work properly, if you undertake to do it at all. "You've got to establish a clear policy about that kind of thing, otherwise it falls into the area of exercises that no one is really prepared to devote enough time and money to. Coming up with a badly prepared proposal for that reason is about the worst disservice you can do your practice."

Although Richard Rogers and Partners still have their hands full with the Lloyds scheme, due to be completed in 1985, they are already looking to a future beyond that. An important role in that respect will very likely be played by a new organisation, Rogers Patscentre Architects, a design research organisation combining the skills of architects and designers with those of a Cambridge group of scientists, PA Technical Service Centre. The idea is that it will tackle the real high-technology problems where engineering and architecture meet and which are now being lost sight of under the stylistic soubriquet of high-tech. Another interesting possibility is that they are occasionally being asked by clients with a lot of cash to invest to find sites and put up schemes for them. That does sound remarkably like by-passing developers, but it could also be part of a trend, noted by Seifert as well, for individually tailored schemes to take the place of the large speculative developments of a decade ago.

An interesting question will be whether they can strike the right balance between the jobs they take on and what they believe to be a manageable size for the practice. In an interview with Denis Sharp in 1979 Rogers was reported as saying that he wanted to keep the limit down to 20–25 architects. At the moment they employ 47 people, but that includes administrative back-up and, somewhat unusually, a team of in-house model-makers. Probably it will be a matter of choosing the work first and then making decisions about staffing levels. "Once you start taking jobs on because you have mouths to feed, it's almost inevitable that you're going to compromise the quality of what you do", Goldschmied says; and it is certainly hard to think of many large practices that have produced a body of work as distinguished and as individual as Richard Rogers and Partners have consistently done over the past twenty years or so.

Robert Matthew, Johnson-Marshall and Partners

Part of our marketing plan was to talk to people outside in the industry about how they saw us. We found we were thought of primarily as public sector architects, in spite of the fact that we've got a large number of major private clients. One of the first things we had to do was to highlight our experience in the private sector.

With about 350 staff spread between major offices in London and Edinburgh, as well as minor ones in several provincial cities and also abroad, RMJM are one of the larger UK practices. They have been going since the 1950s and in that time have developed a formidable array of multi-disciplinary skills—engineering, quantity surveying, interior design and landscape design, as well as architecture and planning. Their work is a roll-call of many of the largest and most prestigious building and planning projects of the last twenty-five years. It embraces all the main building types in many countries, with contract values ranging from £250,000 to over £100m. A great many of them have been around the much sought-after £20m mark—big enough to be rewarding, but not so big as to cause fears of the too-many-eggs-in-one-basket syndrome.

But large though RMJM are, the practice is considerably smaller than it was in the early 70s, when it employed some 600 people. Julian Arkell, a non-architect partner who is in charge of administration, is frank about the fact that the fortunes of the practice—like those of many smaller firms—have been affected by the decline in the public sector. Another problem has been that sheer size has led to some blurring of the identity of what the practice does—the range of its activities and the unifying principles of quality, value for money in design, and effective management that lie behind them. As a first step towards putting this right they have been improving the quality of the material they send out in response to clients' enquiries. This consists of loose-leaf A4 sheets, printed in full colour, which illustrate and briefly describe each major job, and they can be assembled into a package appropriate to what the client wants to know. "You have to respond quickly, and relevantly", says Arkell. It has to be said that the material does not, as yet, include the two items of information which are of most immediate interest to private clients—the extent to which time and cost budgets were met—but this is something they are now working on. They are also improving on the overall graphic presentation and have retained Ken Garland, a graphic designer with a particular interest in architecture, to advise them on that.

One of the first things Garland has done is to devise an RMJM logo. Its simple but also decorative lettering carries a hint of the arts and crafts movement, and that is quite intentional: it is meant to reflect the practice's craftsmanlike approach to the deployment of new materials and technology. Its other purpose is to establish a strongly corporate image for a practice which, like YRM and GMW, has moved away from the personalised partnership of its founders towards something closer to the organisational structure of its main clients. This is one of several reasons why they are in the process of making the transition to becoming a limited company. "It gives you much more flexibility in the way you run things", says Arkell. "With a partnership, a partner has to be involved in every key decision. We still want partners to have that role on the design side, but the day-to-day management of the practice can be put in the hands of directors who are not necessarily partners. The way company accounts are presented is also somewhat clearer and increasingly these days major clients want to see your balance sheet as well as wanting to be satisfied about your human resources." There is also another important advantage: whereas partners are tied, more or less in perpetuity to the liability consequences of the notorious Anns v Merton DC ruling, directors' liability ceases on retirement.

RMJM want to retain some kind of supreme governing body of the last resort, possibly a trust, to hold their numerous offices together and keep the channels of communication open. This is particularly important because of the scale and extent of their overseas operations. They have offices in Tripoli, Riyadh, Dubai, Hong Kong, Singapore and Malaysia. Like other firms who have been successful overseas, their involvement began long before the oil boom, but unlike some they believe in maintaining a physical presence there in spite of the considerable costs. "It's a twenty year commitment, not a quick in and out", is how Arkell describes it. "You have to have a man on the spot who is known and respected locally—and who knows the local culture. How can you build and plan for an environment unless you understand its contexts?" Increasingly, too, overseas clients expect you to train their staff and to effect technology transfer.

We've made some mistakes overseas—who hasn't? The secret, we think, is to pick your spot very carefully—and then to stick with it. Don't try to respond too widely to enquiries that come in.

RMJM have no formal procedures for conducting market research, though. It is up to individual partners to keep up with developments in their particular fields of interest, and the practice library subscribes to the relevant journals. The flow of information is sustained at regular meetings of senior management.

Arkell's own responsibility here lies in doing the basic promotional housekeeping. "It's something which it's easy to overlook unless it's someone's job to take care of it. For instance we think it's important to be in the main directories—not just the RIBA ones, but in the ACA directory, the directory of the British Consultants Bureau which goes out to embassies and consulates abroad, the directories of the main chambers of commerce, *Dun & Bradstreet* and so forth. It's also important to keep our documentation with the RIBA Clients' Advisory Service up to date, though to be honest we haven't found that terribly rewarding as a source of work." Arkell is critical of the present physical environment of CAS. "A rather poky little room adjacent to a clutter of secretarial desks is not likely to inspire the confidence of a major client."

He also has some interesting views on the use of photographs to promote architects' work. They use photographers sparingly and not just for cost reasons.

Architectural photographers tend to produce pictures that will impress other architects or the editors of architectural magazines. I'm not sure that they say enough to non-architectural clients who are not so interested in form, texture and massing. They want something more human and which indicates human scale. How often do you see people in an architectural photograph?

RMJM feel more positive about PR than some firms, probably because they gave their PR man specific assignments, like drafting press releases and articles. But they still feel that the best sources of work come from maintaining and developing contacts with present and prospective clients and also with professionals and consultants in related fields. Some of these come about through the extra-mural activities of members of the practice—teaching, membership of government advisory bodies, in one case a non-executive directorship and, of course, involvement in the RIBA itself. Others come through satisfied clients or through someone seeing their work, and Arkell gives as a case in point the offices they are just completing for the National Farmers' Union Mutual & Avon

Insurance Company. "They came to us because they had seen the Hereford and Worcester County Headquarters we had done—though they also checked us out with the client and the contractor." Some jobs even come through ex-employees. "It's important to keep track of your contacts and maintain your records as they move about. We do a lot of informal lunching, not just as part of our marketing policy but also to bring together people who might be interested in meeting each other."

Sometimes, though not often, client development involves taking on jobs which are smaller than the practice would normally regard as economic. "It's also good for all those on the drawing board to handle something outside their usual run", he believes. "Anyway these days you have to be adaptable and not too rigid, within reason, about the scale of work one takes on."

That adaptability also extends to marketing methods, and RMJM are trying a number of approaches that are new to them. They have just done a "cold" mail shot of a brochure to 1500 large companies, and though it is too early to assess the results, they did get a more positive reaction than some people in the practice had thought might be the case. Another interesting new departure is that they have designed a module for a particular kind of sports facility which a developer is now marketing. They are also now going to developers and similar clients with sites and schemes for them, especially through some of their provincial offices.

They regard this speculative work in a somewhat similar light to entering competitions, though Arkell says that opinions in the practice are somewhat divided about their virtues. "Some of the partners are not too keen, especially on open competitions. You don't get to talk to the client, so you can't really develop a brief with him which bears any relationship to the problem. You're apt therefore to do a lot of work which can be quite off the beam. However, the younger members of the practice are fascinated by them, so we do go in for some, provided they don't clash with more urgent work. They can be quite expensive in both time and money."

But whether or not competitions will become a permanent fact of life, it is now clear that negotiated fees will. RMJM have already had some exposure to them overseas, and in their work in the UK for American multi-national clients. "We got some advice on how to handle that type of client from US-based firms who are good friends of ours and we quoted a lump sum for carefully defined services, with a rate for extras. We find it works very well. We can keep to budget and produce a final certificate of account a few weeks after completion!" The secret, they feel is effective project management, and that is part of the all-round service which they stress to clients they are able to offer, to cost and on time. That is certainly the message private clients want to hear and one feels that RMJM are tackling the difficult problem of re-positioning themselves in the market in a thoughtful way that is likely to continue their successful record over the last twenty-five years.

Rolfe Judd Group Practice

Developers aren't looking for an image—just an architect who knows his job and won't cause them any headaches. I don't think that's at all incompatible with good design.

The quality of Rolfe Judd's buildings as well as of their clients indicates that this is more than just a statement of abstract belief. They are one of the new practices that rose to prominence through the 'seventies, though their beginnings were less then auspicious. David Rolfe and Tony Judd set up the firm in 1968, after they had both been made redundant. They had a network of contacts through friends and people they had worked with—they were careful not to entice clients away from their previous employers—but it took two years before things began to get off the ground. What they mainly had to offer in the first instance was simply professionalism plus hard work. They understood construction techniques and planning procedures and they offered a fast turnround. That meant working often seven days a week and sometimes fourteen hours a day. They even did their own typing in those early difficult days.

Today such pressures are only occasional and they have a staff of 50 and five directors—the practice is set up as an unlimited company—and five managers who are equivalent to associates. But they have never departed from their original principles in getting work. "We're just a couple of ordinary blokes who know the business", says Tony Judd. "We're not flamboyant and right from the time we hired our first employee in 1971 we've been very careful to bring into the practice people we know, like and can work with. That's given us a lot of stability. Only one senior person has left us in all that time to set up on his own—and he's done very well."

When appointing staff, they look, as well as for compatibility with people within the practice, for qualities and attitudes that are likely to be compatible with those of the people in client organisations whom employees of RJGP are likely to be coming into contact with. "We're dealing with professional blokes—property managers, directors, chaps on site. I like to think we have a lot in common with them. The qualities people respond to in their architects are service, know-how, lack of arrogance."

Part of the business of behaving professionally is close attention to lines of communication. Directors always go to meetings, including site meetings. Clients don't want to be fobbed off with more junior ranking people, which is why a lot of big practices lose their way, Tony Judd thinks. It is also important to keep the client informed. "We tell them when we run up against a problem, but we also present the solution—often several solutions—with our recommendations for the optimum one."

Most of their work is in London, where they picked up some important clients in the early seventies while some other architects were concentrating on opportunities in the Middle East to the detriment of their interests in the UK. However they have never gone in for any concerted marketing effort, though they do employ a PR consultant who has been reasonably successful in getting work into the media. They also spend a lot of time and money on their practice brochure. They print only 250 copies and estimate that they cost them £25 each. "That's a lot of money", Tony Judd admits. "But it has to be a quality job, not a throwaway. It has to stand on a desk or be prominent on a shelf. It's a loose-leaf job with a sheet for every building, a brief bit of text and some pictures." It is not sent out as a mail shot, but given personally in reply to specific enquiries.

Their address appears on every sheet, and one mistake they made was that when they moved offices they had to resort to the somewhat untidy expedient of sticking their new address on by hand. Their office is in an attractive and sensitively converted church of the 1830s, with work spaces housed in galleries around an atrium-like central courtyard which serves in part as a staff canteen. They also own a Thames barge which they have converted and keep at St Katherine's Dock for entertaining. Social activities, in fact, are their main form of keeping in touch with clients and other offices outside the professional sphere. The partner biographies in their practice brochure have the unusual but sensible feature of giving details of their hobbies and interests, presumably with the intention of demonstrating to clients that they are not a set of workaholic clones and also of appealing to people with like interests.

In the end, though, getting work still often depends on negotiating skills, though RJGP do not compete on fees directly. "If we cut our fees we also cut our service and we make it clear to clients that's what we're doing."

Sometimes a cut in service or a cost-saving alteration in the design doesn't make any substantial difference to what the client is getting—it's like the difference in what you get between two luxury cars.

They will do a certain amount of work free for a known client in a speculative situation, though they approach this with great caution. They hardly ever do it for a new client, unless he is a blue chip one—but even then they have found that people who want work done for nothing turn out to be bad news in other ways. Tony Judd also says that important clients, coming to the practice for the first time, tend to check them out not only in the matter of professional skills but also for factors like their insurance premium levels and claims records.

RJGP also do some graphic and interior design, but at the moment their interest, in terms of diversification, is focused on the possibility of becoming developers in their own right. They have cut their teeth by acting as developers on their own building. It is owned by the practice's pension fund (as stated earlier, RJGP is an unlimited company) and the company rents it from the fund.

The rental is used to pay off the mortgage, which was raised through ICFC. The pension element is locked into the increasing value of the building. "We didn't read any books on how to do the financial manoeuvres", says Judd. "We picked that up from our clients in the commercial field." The result is in itself a happy advertisement for the skills of the practice as developers, as well as designers.

James Stirling, Michael Wilford & Associates

In the big international competitions there are advantages in even being placed.

"Architects get typecast", says James Stirling, and the typecasting of Stirling, Wilford and Associates, it is fair to say, is that of international superstars. They are probably among the ten best known practices in the world. Work comes to them and they are in the fortunate position of being able to pick and choose the projects that interest them. Perhaps significantly, with the exception of the Tate Gallery Extension, nearly all their work is now abroad: UK clients, one suspects, are nervous of a practice associated with stylistic innovation. Not so in Europe or the USA. Stirling and Wilford are currently working on a DM18m scheme for the Stuttgart State Gallery and another of £5m for the Fogg Museum in Harvard. There is a further job in Italy—the design of a new town—so large that it does not even have a price tag at present. The international spread of their work means that they maintain offices in Stuttgart and Bologna, as well as a base in New York.

Mostly, their jobs come to them through competitions. Their highly distinctive design style would surely transcend anonymity in their entries, and where the jury are favourably disposed towards Stirling's work he must start off with a large advantage. At any rate the practice have had a formidable record of competition success, particularly in Germany.

They have no practice brochure—Stirling refers enquirers

to the many books and the innumerable articles that have been written about his work. Needless to say, he does not have to court the media—journalists come to him and interviews with him are rare. Nevertheless, he admits that there have been leaner times, but his almost unique reputation gives him a simple remedy nowadays. "When work is short," he says. "I simply do more teaching than I normally do."

R. Seifert & Partners

I delegate extensively, but I also make a point of knowing every client personally, so that in the last resort I can help with any problem that has occurred.

Although R. Seifert & Partners is a very large practice, both in numbers—there are 300 employees and ten partners—and of course in its consistently formidable output throughout the post-war era, it is very much the creation of its founder. His ability to strike a balance between delegation and control is an indication of his formidable skills as an administrator, but he believes there is a limit to which they can work effectively. "I think we are about the maximum size at which any kind of personal contact with clients can be maintained." That relationship is very important to him because he believes that the best form of publicity is a satisfied client. "A satisfied client briefs another client", is his view. "Up to now that's the only kind of promotion we've used. I've never chased after work or 'sold' the practice in the way some people are now advocating architecture should be promoted."

In spite of his reputation as an enormously successful developer's architect—he has probably built more of post-1950 London than any other practice—Richard Seifert disapproves of most of the ideas now being promulgated to market the profession. He is, of course, aware of the socio-economic and technological changes that have taken place in recent years and of the necessity for architects to adapt their services to them. "There's less of a tendency for institutions to invest in bricks and mortar on a large scale, though of course they're continuing to build for their own use. There's also a trend towards buying and rehabilitating existing buildings as an investment vehicle. However, big new developments are becoming much scarcer, except on the few prime sites that still come on the market. Developers simply can't raise the necessary finance. Very large developments are now tending to come through consortia of developers who band together to raise the money."

There is, however, a growing trend for the larger developers to use their own in-house architects to run the job itself. Outsiders are used as consultants—maybe to prepare the scheme design or to make presentations to planning committees. For this reason Richard Seifert & Partners have developed areas of special expertise that can be marshalled when a client needs them. Their lavishly produced brochure emphasises the skills of the practice, not only as designers but also in areas like landscape architecture, interior design, project management, model, graphic and video presentation, computer services and environmental services. "We can also bring in experts in areas like cost analysis, energy conservation or fast track construction, either in house or as part of our team", says Seifert. "Being able to respond quickly to specific client requirements seems to me to be more cost effective than having a lot of people on the payroll trying to forecast what those needs might be." The boom areas for his practice at the moment are in hospitals, industrial buildings and new kinds of banking facilities.

Seifert & Partners are often thought of as primarily a UK, even a London-based practice, but in fact they have several offices in the new, resource-rich nations, as well as one in Paris. Competition abroad is often on a fee basis and this has been useful experience in handling the same trend in the UK, though it is one that Richard Seifert disapproves of intensely. "It's pushing architecture into the fish market", he says. "The RIBA's recommended fee scales are increasingly being disregarded." He does not, however, feel any qualms about his practice's ability to handle such situations. "There are construction economies to be achieved by exercising more control over contractors. We've produced our own form of contract to enable us to do that. It embraces aspects of both the JCT and the new ACA contract, though it's different from either of them."

141

Another trend that Colonel Seifert does not greatly care for is the competitive interview as a method of selection. "We have to go along with it, but it tends to over-simplify complex problems. Solutions have both a financial and an architectural dimension. They need more study than a competitive interview gives scope for." He feels there are similar difficulties over the increasingly popular form of competition where a developer makes a joint submission with an architect—for instance the National Gallery competition. "You're trying to satisfy two different, though related, sets of criteria competitively. That's a very difficult thing to do, and I think accounts for the difficulties that have arisen over that particular competition."

Seifert & Partners go in for a lot of competitions, particularly abroad, but their large output has never been associated with any particular stylistic attachment. He himself seems to be more interested in the impact of technology on architecture than ideology. For instance he sees a move back towards indigenous materials in construction. He feels that his own resistance to buildings that are the product of ideological positions or "statements" of various kinds is reflected in the attitudes of his clients. "What people want is a building that is worth the money they paid for it." An important part of proving that you can achieve that objective is to keep a tight control on costs. "We pride ourselves on the fact that the fee we say we're going to charge—which is based on the contract—is the final amount. In fact, we sometimes manage to build for less than the contract, in which case we give the difference back to the client."

The importance of mastering the web of planning regulations which looms so large in the comments made by many architects is something that Seifert makes curiously little of, in view of his reputation in that respect. "Yes, I know the planning laws, but that's part of knowing your business. It's up to every architect to study the regulations and come up with the same conclusions that I have."

Francis Weal & Partners

You have to respond to an enquiry quickly, be on the site the same afternoon, come up with a sketch proposal the next morning. I did that recently with a community project for some workshops. Nothing came of it, but my name was passed on to some potential clients I'm now talking to.

When Francesca Weal was told by one of the principals in the firm she was working in at the time that women make jolly good assistants but aren't really partner material she decided to set up on her own. In preparation for that step she began doing some moonlighting, but then a happy opportunity presented itself to step into a ready-made architectural *pied à terre*. Her father is also an architect and he decided to move to Hampshire—but he also wanted to keep the London end of his practice going. He had kept the top floor of a mansion in south London as a base, and Francesca Weal moved in there to take over a workload which had been thin for a while but had the potential to expand, with a number of larger projects which were about to come on stream. They consisted mainly of housing association work, flats for the elderly and a number of jobs for the Catholic Church. The challenge was to expand the potential and existing workload and to broaden the base of the practice. In that sense, though she was taking over an existing practice, Francesca Weal's task has been similar to starting from scratch.

She was however fortunate in being able to build on some pretty solid long-established connections—particularly those with the Church. "The Church sells parcels of land every now and then, and that is a possible opportunity for another batch of my clients, namely housing associations", she explains. "They need a sympathetic vendor because in purely commercial terms the opinion up to now has been that you can make more money selling land to a developer, provided the site is suitable."

Her main clients in fact are still housing associations. "The only problem is that they're dependent on getting finance from the Housing Corporation", she says. "They can't pay your fee until the project is approved and the land has been purchased. In one case the production drawings were well under way before we could place our fee account and there's always the risk of doing a lot of work for nothing." However, she is resigned to the fact that this is an inevitable aspect of practice, especially in working with housing associations, and that even a proposal that comes to nothing can ultimately lead to something more positive.

It is also something you have to face with private clients. She did a lot of work on the proposed conversion and extension of a cricket pavilion for which she never got a fee—but she did get a lot of useful experience and "an awful lot of free drinks". In the early days, in fact, she found her local pub quite a rich source of information for leads and promising contacts. Now she relies more on a mixture of reading papers like the *Estates Gazette*, keeping her ears open when talking to clients—Catholic priests can be a good source of news about highly secular matters—and her eyes peeled when she is driving around London. After that, it is a question of alerting suitable clients like housing associations about possible sites, and of keeping up with changes in the market. She has noticed, for instance, that commercial developers are taking an increased interest in one of her specialities—sheltered housing for the elderly.

News of trends such as this filters through to conferences and seminars, and in spite of the time—and money—they take up she finds it worthwhile attending them, especially those connected with housing associations.

A small but growing number of the associations' professional staff are women. "I can't say there's any kind of feminist Mafia anywhere but as women move into more senior positions something like it could develop. But I'm not counting on it, any more than I'm counting on the Cambridge Mafia as a source of work. I only qualified three years ago and only one of my contemporaries has emerged as a potential client. He already had a background in commercial development and we have been getting together packages for land bids on a speculative basis."

She has a number of contracts going through at the moment ranging from £60,000 to £1m but she has not yet had time to produce a practice brochure. For the time being she is relying on sending out the RIBA Practice Index Form to enquirers, having put the details into the word processor she shares with a firm of quantity surveyors downstairs. On the other hand she does go to the considerable expense of having her buildings professionally photographed. These photographs then form part of her client presentation, but in some cases the clients who approach her are uncomfortably small. "Advertising in local directories and in the yellow pages is a waste of time", she has found. "It's not normally worth our while doing anything with a contract value of less than £20,000, though we do do some smaller projects for personal friends and for people who are also larger clients in other ways. For instance we did some fire damage work for that reason." But in general she says that people who come in off the street because they have seen your name in a directory are not a viable source of work if you have an office to support. They are also the ones who quibble most vociferously about fees. Of the other clients for whom she does small jobs, she says, "the biggest problem is that they sometimes don't know precisely what they want—for instance, how extensive a rehab job will have to be, whether they can afford to have it done all at once, in stages or what." In such cases she has found the best course is to make a time charge with the option of switching to a percentage fee when more is known.

She has her name down with the Clients' Advisory Service

The Architects

but it has produced nothing yet. On the whole she finds that help comes to those who help themselves. "I try to keep in touch with clients—to meet them face to face whenever I can. For instance the clergy love to see you and though these are essentially social calls, if anybody has any interesting information from a professional point of view, they tend to tell you about it."

Sometimes, though, sheer luck plays a part—especially if you help it along. She came across the Cambridge contemporary already referred to because he had seen a building he liked that had been signed by the practice and he followed it up. "He didn't associate me with Francis Weal & Partners at all, but of course it helped when we found we already knew each other." She now thinks that they should always sign their buildings. "Anything ethical that might catch the attention of a potential client—and anyone who is interested in who built what comes into that category—is worth doing—particularly if it costs nothing."

John Winter & Associates

I'd be delighted to design a dormer window for your house. I've never seen the charm of bigness.

To what extent the first part of that comment was meant to be taken literally could perhaps be a matter of conjecture, but certainly John Winter means what he says when it comes to the size of his office. Amazingly for such a prestigious, highly publicised firm he operates essentially as a one-man band, though at one time he had fourteen people working in his office. It was then in Covent Garden, but he moved out when rents went from £2 to £14 a square foot, taking with him the five other firms who have long been associated, though not directly connected with him.

They are all design professionals of one sort or another, ranging from a graphic designer to a company that organises architectural tours. Their paths crossed in Winter's progress from being an Architectural Association teacher operating a small practice out of the AA—the teaching income and the availability of a phone and a central London address was a great help in getting things going—to practicing more or less full-time.

The "more or less" is important. John Winter has an active career as a teacher and writer as well as being an architect and doesn't believe that a full-time commitment to any one thing produces the best work. "Ideally no one should work at architecture more than four days a week", he says. "Putting up buildings is only one aspect of the job." That attitude is echoed by the people with whom he shares his premises—they all teach and write as well as practice. They share a workspace (a converted ice-cream factory) because of the stimulus they give each other—there is very little cross-fertilisation as far as actual jobs are concerned. "We've all been together for twenty years", Winter says. "We share ideas and problems. It also means that we can afford resources like secretarial services and a library which would probably be beyond our means as individuals."

John Winter's jobs may be small scale, but there are a lot of them. They embrace private houses, rehabilitation and conversion, small industrial buildings and quite a lot of local authority and housing association commissions. A major client is the Borough of Camden, and that was the motive for locating the office in that part of London. But many of his clients are private individuals who live in the area and who range from affluent Hampstead trendies to ordinary working people who come in through the door from the surrounding local authority estates and are nowadays often buying the house in which they have been council tenants. Winter never fails to give advice, though if the job is too small he would refer the caller to an appropriately sized practice or to a suitable moonlighter. He also says that you have to be realistic and refer jobs that are too big. "We were asked to do all the working drawings for a new hospital in Hong Kong, but I felt it was simply too much for a practice my size and passed it on to someone bigger."

Apart from the kind of enquiries which come more or less out of the blue, work emanates from a variety of sources. Quite a lot comes through the Clients' Advisory Service, some from estate agents (Winter has a high public profile in the Hampstead area) and some from developers. In some ways he finds working with them easier than with housing associations. "Developers generally know what they want and are clear about expressing it. Housing associations tend to be amorphous as clients and some of their technical officers can be difficult to deal with." He found conditions easier in the 'seventies, when he himself helped to set up some housing associations. Changes in the law now no longer allow building professionals to get work from associations when they are on the management committee.

An interesting and apparently important part of Winter's

contact network are architectural photographers. He always has his buildings photographed by one of the top professionals and they themselves are in contact in the course of their work with people who are potential clients. But by far the most significant part of the network are private individuals for whom he has built or rehabilitated a house. "When they sell, they tend to recommend us to the purchasers. When they buy another house that needs work done on it, they turn to us." He rings up the owners when he hears that one of "his" houses is on the market.

Our previous clients are our best source of work, direct and indirect. I'd be shattered if I lost a client.

That kind of close, almost familial relationship means that Winter takes on some very small jobs indeed: he quotes as an example a £4500 farmhouse in Yorkshire, where the owner had simply seen and liked other work he had done nearby. That, of course, is below normal economic size, but the job interested him. He likes the challenge of newness. That may range from a geographical determinant—he has built houses as far apart as Buffalo in upstate New York and Dijon in France—to a building type that is new to him, like a farm or a recording studio for a pop group.

The range of his work is difficult to encapsulate in a brochure and instead he keeps extensive photographic records from which client presentations can be assembled. he also has a scrap book of articles about his work—he gets good coverage in some upmarket consumer magazines like *House & Garden* which is useful for an architect who does what these days is an unusual amount of private house design.

Strangely enough, in spite of the high reputation of his practice he is not a great believer in going in for competitions. The process runs counter to his design philosophy. "In my work the actual design emerges quite late in the course of meetings and discussions when you try to get to what the right solution is from the client's point of view. With a competition you start from the wrong end."

The unity that emerges from the diversity of Winter's architecture lies in the importance he attaches to getting the client involved in the process of design. It is a time-consuming commitment—he reckons he spends about five evenings a week with them. But it seems to be the viewpoint that determines the directions in which he looks for work. To support it he quotes a remark by Bruce Goff:

I'd like to design the sort of house the client would design if he were a great architect.

YRM

Clients these days are much better informed and there's less spec building by developers in the hope of an occupant. Generally an occupant exists or has been signed up and he has a clear set of objectives about time, cost and how he wants the building to perform.

Architectural practices tend to have a character somewhere between an atelier and a management consultant. YRM leans towards the latter end of that spectrum, but the contraction of their name to the initials of their founders (Yorke, Rosenberg & Mardall) was not intended to give them a suitably corporate image. The original partners were, however, concerned that there were very few examples of highly personalised practices forming a successful second generation. The name YRM is a slot into which future partners could fit while retaining a recognisable link with past achievements.

These achievements have been considerable. YRM have been continuously successful since they were founded just after the war by F. R. S. Yorke. They now employ 250 people and tackle some very large jobs indeed—up to £250m in contract value. Bryan Henderson, now the senior partner, is very much aware of the problems of internal as well as external communication that arise when a practice grows to that size. "We've broken it down into a number of divisions dealing with particular aspects—for instance we have YRM Engineering, YRM Interiors and YRM International. When these divisions have an internal meeting there's always a partner present. Then we have divisional director meetings once a month with a formal agenda. The partners also meet formally once a month."

Although some of the divisions have fairly different

functions from each other, Henderson has rejected the idea of turning them into separate profit centres. "There are some advantages to that from the point of view of accounting-based controls, but it can also produce attitudes where units within the firm won't co-operate with each other because they can't see any 'profit' in it."

One reason why that would be particularly damaging is that the various divisions have to co-operate to study the needs of a prospective client. Identifying those needs and putting forward a solution to them is a vital part of getting work these days. The other, equally vital element is to be able to demonstrate that you can manage the contract efficiently and finish it to a programme. The root of the problem, Henderson thinks, is the historically adversarial relationship between architects and contractors. YRM are changing that by establishing themselves as management contractors. "That helps us sort out all the potential contractor problems beforehand instead of being faced with a long list of variations and claims after the event", he says. Incidentally that kind of complete contract management operation enables YRM to earn higher fees as well as do, in Henderson's view, a more efficient job than is possible in the conventional architect/client relationship. "Design is still important, of course, but clients are suspicious of arty solutions that turn out to be difficult to build and to raise all kinds of cost problems."

Part of the increasing professionalism and awareness that he is finding among clients is the fact that they expect the architect to talk about their problems with some degree of understanding. Though YRM do no formal market research as such, he and his fellow senior partner David Alford do keep themselves informed by reading such publications as the *Financial Times*, the *Economist* and so forth. Likewise clients read the professional press and YRM employ a small PR section and have sponsored a book about the practice. The chief value of coverage in architectural magazines, however, is that they get quite a lot of work through other architects. "We might, for instance, be approached by a local architect who's been given a large local commission—there's an increasing amount of regional bias in these matters, to encourage local enterprise and provide local employment. Quite often such firms come to us as partners, because they haven't the resources to do the job. I might say that we are also sometimes the junior partners in such enterprises." Henderson gives as examples the US Embassy which they did with Saarinen in the fifties and more recently the Boots HQ with SOM. Another source of work are in-house architects in client organisations:

Often in-house architects have a rather low status in the hierarchy that employs them. How often do you hear of an architect becoming a director of a public company? Nurturing them carefully—even flatteringly—can be highly productive.

Competitions are another source of work, but YRM stick to invited, limited-entry ones. "Open competitions tend to attract far too large an entry, including people who don't have much work and students and academics who have access to free resources. For a practice with a large workload and large overheads open competitions are very expensive—it can cost £40,000–£50,000."

In one way or another, though, competition plays an increasing role in getting work. Sometimes it is implied, as in the case of selection by competitive interview. YRM spend a lot of money on presentations in such cases and, unusually, try to find out the reason when they have not been appointed if they think they should have got the job. "The truth, if you can get it, can be very instructive for the next time around", says Henderson. There is also competition on fees: YRM don't cut corners to keep prices down, but quoting a rock bottom figure means that you can't do more than you are paid to do. "I don't think it's a healthy development", he says. "It goes against the grain of how architects think and are trained."

Like many other architects, he believes that doing good

153

work is ultimately the most effective way of getting and holding clients. As a token of their commitment to what they design they always sign their buildings. They also regard their own office, which they developed themselves, as a continuing advertisement for the practice and they spend a lot of money on apparently minor things like flowers and graphics for internal stationery. "It's these little things that can add up to a big impression."

Part 2
The Clients

Capital & Counties Public Company Ltd

It's essential that the architect must have an appreciation of how developers work and that a good relationship grows up. On the size of projects that we do we might have to work with a firm over a period of years with our project manager and their job architect meeting on the site every day.

As a major client with several projects and schemes on the go or in the pipeline at the same time a developer has to strike a balance between working with practices with whom he is familiar and keeping a look-out for new talent. Thus although there are close relationships between certain developers and certain architects, this by no means precludes a new firm from getting into the act, especially with a client as large as Capital & Counties, whose range includes major shopping centres, commercial offices and industrial building as well as housing (through their subsidiary, Roger Malcolm Homes).

The process by which architects are selected has, however, become much more rigorous since the comfortable days when it was sufficient to know the right people on the developer's board. Not, of course, that the social dimension has disappeared entirely. "What often happens is that I go to some contractor's 'do' and the host will put me next to an architect of whom he thinks highly," says Brian Jolly, managing director of Capital & Counties. That however is only a part of a continuing and wide-ranging programme of keeping track of people Capital & Counties might some day want to work with. "We get quite a lot of information about

The Clients

architects from QSS and other building professionals", says Jolly, explaining the process. "When that happens we might get them in for lunch, go and look at their offices and tour around some of their buildings. Firms of chartered surveyors are a source of information as well."

The most reliable way of validating competence, though, is actually to have worked with the architect in question. Capital & Counties keep a record of people they have worked with and what they think of them and this applies not only to the principals in the firms concerned but also to their key staff.

General intelligence about architects is particularly useful because sometimes developers are thrown together with them almost by force of circumstance. For instance there may be a site on the market for which planning permission has been granted subject to a particular scheme being built on it which has already been designed by the vendor's architect. The question then is whether the firm is one that Capital & Counties can work with. It may also happen that the situation is less clearly defined: permission is not tied to a particular design, but the architect has already put in a lot of work with the planning authorities. That leaves the purchasing developer with the option of paying him off or going ahead with him. More commonly, though, the initiative comes from Capital & Counties. "We have a site in mind or offered to us where planning permission is subject to a suitable scheme being devised", explains Brian Jolly. "So we ask an architect to produce a design for us. That would be on a time charge with a ceiling. We used to work on a 'no cure, no pay' basis, but we came to the conclusion that wasn't a good idea. Among other drawbacks, it creates a sense of obligation, no matter how hard-headed one tries to be about it." Another method of producing designs for planning permission is of course, to organise a limited competition where Capital & Counties pay the costs of invited entrants.

Brian Jolly has noticed some increase in the number of practices who approach them with schemes as the implications of the changes in the Code are absorbed. "Some of the

Capital & Counties Public Company Ltd

more aggressive ones nowadays keep an eye on the *Estates Gazette* and contact us if there's a site we might be interested in", he says. "It's a good idea if that's the road you want to follow, to get hold of the company reports of developers, look at their stuff and see who's who." Capital & Counties have an unusually informative brochure about themselves.

Getting hold of the right person in the organisation can be quite important. It's a question of trying to focus on their interests, responsibilities, personal predilections and so forth. Saying "I know your MD*" is often counter-productive—even if you do.*

Working with a developer is not something that suits those architects who continue to have an uncompromising view of themselves as leaders of the building team. Capital & Counties employ their own project managers, and Brian Jolly sees the role of the architect as being that of providing the overall concept rather than the management aspects of it. "He shouldn't even be designing the window sills—the builder can do that", he says. However, the rewards of winning the trust of a large developer can be considerable. Jolly mentions that a scheme like the Victoria Centre shopping scheme in Nottingham took ten years to complete. The stability that such continuity offers also leaves a practice scope to range wider in search of more varied work. Indeed developers welcome that kind of initiative, creating as it does the balance between new ideas and experience that they look for in their architects.

Book Club Associates

The Clients' Advisory Service came up with the names of three firms. We chose Moxley Jenner & Partners because we felt there were three vital areas where our interests needed to be protected—the performance specification of the building, construction time and cost. The thing that swayed us in their favour was that they had a QS partner in the practice.

Book Club Associates are typical of the more sophisticated clients who come to the RIBA for advice; that is to say that they are a substantial, well-managed firm (they are Britain's largest book club), aware of the difference that a good architect can make but not a regular user of architectural services, and therefore without established contacts in the profession. In 1978 they found they needed to build a new warehouse. The chosen location was Swindon and the building had to accommodate eight million books in 180,000 square feet of storage and packing space. They lined up funding with a developer. The contract value was around £6m on the basis of a fixed sum, plus variations.

They had employed specialist warehouse consultants in the early stages of the project, but decided not to retain them for the construction phase. The consultants had, however, made some valuable suggestions, and one that BCA took particular notice of was that they should employ their own project manager and clerk of works on the building. The developer would, of course, have his own project manager on the job, but BCA were advised that in the event of argument or disputes that person would inevitably take the side of his employer—not that of BCA. Michael Armstrong, the administrative director of the book club was also aware of the "bid low, claim high" syndrome.

It was with this problem that he approached CAS and once

Moxley Jenner had been appointed they worked out a very precise performance specification for the building and agreed it with the developer. Thereafter, Moxley Jenner were constantly on hand to check progress, keep track of costs and sort out disputes—always on the grounds of whether or not claims were reasonable in the light of what the performance specification had called for. "For instance we successfully disputed a claim for £42,000 for adjustments to the heating levels on the grounds that the ones being produced didn't match what had been previously agreed", Armstrong says. BCA spent £300,000 on fees to their own consultants and felt that it was worth every penny.

The only problem had been that they had had no control over the sub-contractors, so when the book club moved offices in London and needed to convert the building they were going into, they engaged Moxley Jenner to act as architects and project managers. Ray Moxley recommended that the job should be done by direct professional control and that this would ensure a tighter fit of purpose building at a lower cost. So it proved. The architects engaged their own sub-contractors—in fact one of the major ones was sacked in the course of the job—and though there was a serious over-run on one cost element, this was more than balanced by demonstrable savings in other areas.

The experience has won Michael Armstrong over to the idea of using project managers for BCA's future work. In fact he has extended the concept to his private work. When his own house was partly burnt out last winter he got a project manager to supervise the repairs—not an architect because the job was not big enough to attract one. He learnt a lesson on that—though possibly there is also a lesson for the profession in the fact that a small private client can also be a large corporate one in another *persona*. "The project manager let through a claim of £37 on a variation for a job that I know from my own experience couldn't have taken more than 10 minutes. I'm very much in favour of the idea of project management—but you have to have a good, tough one to make it work."

Harding Housing Association

We take up references from architects' previous clients. What we have to look for mainly, now that funds are short, is the ability to work within the limits laid down for housing associations in the tables of total indicative costs.

The Harding Housing Association in south London regards itself as "smallish", but how relative that adjective is can be seen from the size of its operations. It controls 900 units and a £24m housing stock. As a potential client Harding is quite sizeable, but it is indeed small in comparison to such giants as the Notting Hill Housing Association, which controls some 4000 units.

Housing associations in general have become significant sources of work in recent years and have largely taken over the role of local authorities in the housing field. As a hybrid between a private and a public sector client, their methods are more diverse than those of local authorities but Harding is fairly typical in both the nature and scale of its operations. It was started in 1968 by a Dr Beryl Harding to fill the gap for people who could neither get council housing nor afford the private variety. With funding from the local authority the association bought up properties that no one else wanted and used improvement grant money to do them up for letting. They still do not allow tenants to buy properties—although some associations now do and are in fact operated on a profit-making basis. Harding, on the other hand, is a registered charity and by that token, non-profit making, though they, like other associations, are tougher than the local authorities about dealing with non-paying tenants.

Some of the association's funds come through the GLC, but

mostly they derive through the Housing Corporation; and they are made available for a variety of purposes, including rehabilitation, maintenance, improvement, and for new buildings. Harding were beginning to be quite active in this latter sphere, but it is the one that has been most severely affected by government cutbacks. Nevertheless they own a number of houses that were put up as new buildings, including a £500,000 group of flats for the elderly.

With new buildings the association is not confined to its area, SW18, as it is in the case of other work. Another restriction is that 50 per cent of the tenants are nominated by the local authority, but by far the most rigorous one relates to the costs of work done. In the case of rehab, there is a table of Total Indicative Costs—the money available for various ranges of floor areas and occupancy rates—from which the purchase price has to be deducted. There are also maintenance grants of £90 per unit at present.

The running of the Association, the supervision of building works and the selection of outside professionals is in the hands of a paid staff, which in the case of Harding consists of 14 people. It includes a qualified building surveyor and there is also a manager with experience in the industry who looks after the maintenance side. The rest are primarily administrative people. Consequently they rely heavily on outside architects and contractors. Their spokesman admits that the paperwork involved in dealing with a housing association can be formidable. "You also have to be pretty strong on the supervision side", he adds. "The job is not regarded as completed until the end of a six-month maintenance period." These rules are laid down in a thick volume which provides the basis for the brief: *The Schematic Procedure Guide*. Design aspects are laid down in another thick volume—*Design and Contract Criteria*.

At one time architects and other building professionals were on the boards of housing associations, but now no-one who has a possible beneficial interest in work is allowed to hold such a position. Perhaps for this reason some architects

The Clients

have shown less interest in housing association work in recent years. Harding report that they get some approaches from practices who have found suitable sites or properties—but not many. They get more proposals from estate agents and, of course, they look for sites themselves.

Are architects right to have cooled somewhat towards housing association work as the snags have shown themselves—complicated administrative procedures, slow payment and (in some cases) awkward in-house staff with a little, dangerous knowledge of architectural matters? Harding—and a good many architects who have found housing associations a fruitful source of work—think not. "Yes, we've been badly hit by cutbacks", their spokesman says. "But the need for housing won't go away and the trend will continue for it to be supplied by housing associations. Both the main political parties are committed to that."

Greycoat Estates Ltd

Chiefly we look for design excellence—easier to recognise than to define. But we also look for sheer technical skill. It's absolutely vital with the high-tech materials and construction methods that are used on our buildings for a practice to have a thorough understanding of engineering and servicing problems, as well as of the economic implications of various construction solutions.

An appraisal process as thorough as this clearly calls for something much more prolonged and detailed than a tour round a practice's office and a visit to their buildings. Geoffrey Wilson, chief executive of Greycoat Estates, does not appoint architects *ad hoc* to a particular scheme, but keeps several practices in his sights—sometimes over a period of years—until the right building comes along for one or other of the firms with whom he builds up a continuing relationship. During the course of that time, Greycoat will try to build up an understanding of that practice's philosophy and look at how they work—who does what and which skills they can muster in design, administration and the technological know-how which he refers to in his introductory quote.

Apart from an intense awareness of the importance of quality in all aspects of the building process, Wilson's attitude also reflects a great personal interest in architecture. Pride of place among the pictures in his expensively but unostentatiously furnished office is given to a very attractive small pencil drawing—a perspective with a plan tucked away in a corner—of a late arts and crafts villa by an unknown Edwardian architect. Wilson picked it up for 1/6d in a junk shop some years ago. It is hardly what you would expect in the office of one of the country's major developers, whose projects include not only the controversial Coin Street site where Richard Rogers is the architect, but Cutlers Gardens (with Richard Seifert), the new Victoria Plaza (with Elsom, Pack & Roberts), Finsbury Avenue (with Arup Associates), an office block in Hammersmith (with Michael Lyle Associates) and a modest redevelopment at 65 Brook Street (with the Rolfe Judd Group Practice). But then Geoffrey Wilson rejects the traditional image, which some architects still cling to, of the developer as a promoter whose principal interest is in getting the largest lettable area for the least cost. This view, he believes, has at least in the recent past caused some of the best UK architects to turn their backs on "commercial" architecture and to prefer more prestigious public sector or academic work.

Even now, Greycoat Estates, who have a reputation as being one of the classiest as well as one of the most successful British developers, seldom get approached by architects who want to work with them. Mostly the initiatives come from Greycoat, and spread around their foyer are all the major architectural magazines, as well as the real estate ones and those concerned with business and economics in general. It is from the perusal of these magazines as well as in visiting exhibitions and attending architectural occasions of various kinds that Wilson begins to mark his card—and his search is not confined to the up-and-coming names who are already widely known. He has even been sighted at the AA's annual summer exhibition.

Wilson does not, however, subscribe to the idea that architects should be leaders of the construction team. That he believes to be Greycoat's role, and they would choose and orchestrate the various professional consultants. He would not even necessarily employ the architect to do all the design. "We don't think the architects of a building are necessarily also the right people to design the interior", he says. "There's a certain sameness about architects' tastes. You can pretty much guarantee, for instance, that every architect's office will have a Mies chair or an Eames chair or somehow be following the latest architectural magazine fashion. We see the architect as a key member of the creative team, but not as its indisputable leader."

Wilson's attitude to the financial aspects of development is rather similar. Profit plays a key role but it is not absolutely paramount. "If an architect came to us with a prime site for which he had planning permission we wouldn't give him the job unless we were convinced of the quality of his work." However he does believe in the importance of the marketplace as being the ultimate test of whether a project works, and he is firm about architects having to accept that. By way of illustrating the point he tells the story of a very distinguished firm whose project—much written up in architectural magazines at the time—was never built because their design imposed impossible conditions on the key tenant. "They wanted a prestige office built by a top architect, but it was part of the architect's vision that in design terms the occupants should be anonymous. It was a multi-million pound project—not the sort of thing that even a famous practice can lightly afford to lose. But lose it they did."

How does Wilson see the future of the environment in which architects will be looking for work? There has, for instance, been a lot of criticism of his own Coin Street development on the grounds that it is adding further office space at a time when the need for it is shrinking. He disputes that. "The spaces that are unlettable are the ones that were build in the 'sixties for a forty-year life span. What we are building are offices for the 'eighties and 'nineties. What is needed now are spaces that are flexible, have low running costs, fewer individual occupants and can be modified quite drastically at intervals which may be as short as ten years." Awareness of what is, rather than insistence on a vision of what ought to be is the crucial factor in getting work. "Designing a building is like designing a plane. It's got to fly and operate economically. Good intentions and good design are not enough by themselves."

Debenham Tewson & Chinnocks

Without wishing to be swamped by architects phoning me up or sending me literature, I should point out that we are looking all the time for ways to invest our clients' money.

Debenham, Tewson & Chinnocks' geographical location close by St Paul's is an indication of their close ties to the City, though these days they also have offices or associates in the continent of Europe, in the USA, Australia and the Middle and Far East. They are one of the largest and most respected of those British firms whose expertise in the use, management and development of land has become an important source of invisible earnings as well as playing a highly significant role on the UK financial scene. To define their position more precisely, their brochure shows their activities as embracing: development and project management, agency (sale and acquisition), advice on the deployment of real estate investment, property and portfolio management, building law, taxation and planning advice, building surveys and valuation.

It follows that one of their key concerns is to advise their clients on the selection of architects. R. B. Caws, the senior partner, explains that in a new development the steps are that first his firm begins by estimating its value as a finished project and the costs that will be incurred along the way to that goal. They then choose an architect who will produce a design that will fetch those values within the limits of the estimated costs. Increasingly their services are being called in to the Middle East, where property owners are beginning to realise that in the building boom of the 'seventies huge costs were incurred without much thought as to the longer term values which would be created. They are also being brought into the non-commercial sector by housing associations—particularly in cases of mixed commercial/residential developments.

There, as in many other situations, quite sensitive planning and environmental considerations are often involved. "We may recommend a consultant architect to handle the design and a more commercial firm to provide the project management", Caws says. "Ideally, of course, we'd like the design and management aspects handled competently within the same practice." It does happen, but Caws believes that all but the most skilled, tough and experienced practices are handicapped by the JCT Contract, which makes it very difficult for the architect to keep a grip on the builder. He thinks the new ACA Contract might be more successful in that respect. But he also says that architects themselves are often to blame when things go awry. "They're very bad at deciding at an early stage what they finally want and rely on variation orders to get it right", he has found. That, he feels, is unfair on the client—and could be grotesquely so in the days of percentage fees, because the more the building cost, the higher the architect's fee went. The abolition of the mandatory fee scale has had the effect that he and most other surveyors now call for a fixed-fee tender; but they still insist that the contractor must be supplied with all the drawings before he tenders.

The move towards splitting the design of a scheme and management of the building phase does not, however, diminish the architect's responsibility for seeing that what he designed actually gets built. Caws has a note of warning here on the matter of job architects:

It's essential to have a good job architect—otherwise the design may never be realised.

For this reason he pays a great deal of attention to the depth of talent in a practice in making his selection. "The flair and talent is in individuals, not in the name of the practice. It's a point some famous firms tend to forget. Sometimes a name comes up in our discussions and you find someone saying, 'Yes, they were good in the 'sixties, but who's there now?' Bringing in new blood and new ideas is absolutely vital."

Very interestingly, he points out that this business of not relying on past achievements also applies to newer practices. "You can make a big name with some building and then run out of steam", he says. "We have to look for consistent quality. If a firm is lucky enough to do a building that gets into all the papers, they ought, after that, to get back to basics—take on small jobs, do some work-a-day stuff. You can't rely on acclaim lasting indefinitely." On the other hand he admits that it does have its advantages. "In a sensitive site, you might choose a big name architect because that's who the minister who makes the ultimate decision will have heard of."

The final method of choice is, of course, increasingly by competition. He says that this is a slow process, though not as slow as open competitions, which for that reason he thinks should only be used for very important sites. The fact that architects enter particularly open competitions without advice from surveyors and other building professionals means that their submissions are often unbuildable. In fact this often happens, even with the winner's entry, if the composition of the jury is not sufficiently practical. As an example Caws points to one highly publicised recent competition—"I guarantee you that the finished building will look nothing like the winning design."

In his constant search for new architectural talent, Caws keeps a close eye on what is happening in the profession and looks at brochures that are sent to him—not only from the point of view of what the buildings in them look like, but whether they were finished on time and to budget. He finds that brochures do not pay enough attention to that side of things. As yet, however, he has had relatively few direct approaches from architects as a result of the relaxations in the Code of Conduct.

This is somewhat surprising, because he wears two other important hats in addition to that of senior partner in Debenham Tewson & Chinnocks. He is chairman of the property committee of the New Towns Commission—the role of the Commission is to take over the management of new towns from the corporation once they are established. The Commission chooses projects and selects architects for work in the new towns. "We do get initiatives from local architects—small firms who know the sites. They come along with schemes and ideas. I think it's perhaps easier to grasp the starting point in new towns than in established sites surrounded by the claims of various planning interests." His other hat is that of one of the eight Crown Estate Commissioners who look after land directly owned by the monarch, something which is quite separate from what the PSA does. "Since the time of George III the monarch has given up income from this land in exchange for the Civil List", he explains. It includes some highly important sites in central London as well as in some lesser known areas in the provinces. Work tends to be distributed among 20–30 well-known practices on the basis of limited competitions.

In the nature of his duties, Caws is exposed to a great number of architectural presentations. "I'm not really all that swayed by very elaborate ones, though I agree that in the Middle East they are effective—even necessary. Here the feeling is that you end by paying indirectly for presentations on which the architect has clearly spent a lot of money." His requirements are straightforward, sensible—and so obvious that they might get overlooked. "What I really want to know is who is in the practice, what their background is and whether they can show me that they have a record of finishing work on time and to cost. I'm also interested in how they are likely to be received by the planners and what their general philosophy is." He stresses that this does not require anything elaborate in the way of audio-visual technology. "I've been most impressed by people like Freddie Gibberd and Sir Hugh Casson. Freddie Gibberd used to give presentations with no written material at all—he just brought along his drawing materials." He admits that such an approach might not work with every client these days, but it enshrines a basic principle which is still valid.

The ability of an architect to think graphically on his feet in front of an audience is still probably the most valuable gift he can bring to bear in a presentation.

Talking about presentations further, Caws also thinks that it would be valuable for firms to try to find out why they did not get appointed. "We do that ourselves. Clients seldom give you the whole truth, but you can often pick up enough hints to make the exercise worthwhile. Post mortems on why you won can also be useful, of course."

As far as the future is concerned, he believes that the system of developers calling for a package fixed-fee deal from a group of professionals—who are then left to sort out among themselves how the money is apportioned—is here to stay. He also thinks that competing on price will be a growing trend. "Architects have nothing to fear from that", he maintains. "If they know their costs, which they certainly should."

Like many others, he does not believe that architects are suited by temperament or training to be developers. "Only about half the schemes put to us by architects make any commercial sense", he has found. "Architects don't understand the first law of development which is that the value created must fund the cost of the building and make a profit. I'd advise any architect who wants to get into development to at least team up with a QS and a chartered surveyor who is qualified in the valuation of buildings." Coming from a senior chartered surveyor that may sound like an unsurprising recommendation, but it is also supported by a great number of architects who have been examining this new option now open to them.

Property Services Agency

I look at magazines, competitions and at buildings which I've heard are interesting. I might say "have you looked at so and so's work?" to the Director making the final choice.

This comment by Geoff Woodward, Acting Director of Design Services at the PSA—in other words its acting architectural overlord—explains the role of the man who is certainly the biggest single client in the UK. It is to guide and advise those who actually appoint outside architects, rather than to take a hand in that process himself. Indeed the enormous scope of the PSA's work would virtually preclude that because its major projects alone have an annual contract value of about £500m—leaving out a lot of minor stuff at UK regional level. A large proportion of that work is military and diplomatic, though during the 'seventies a considerable chunk of it was for British Telecom's programme of revitalisation. Since then the overall value of work has declined slightly, though the share going to outside consultants has actually increased to 60 per cent and Woodward thinks it will probably grow to two thirds. Patronage on that scale has increased consciousness of the PSA's power to impose design standards on outside consultants as well as of the importance of maintaining its own internal ones. In the 'seventies, PSA set up two monitoring bodies. The Design Office keeps an eye on in-house design, management and contract procedures. The Design Panel's role is to look at schemes being submitted and to conduct post mortems on built projects. It includes some non-PSA architects; for instance Ted Happold and Sir Anthony Cox have served on it.

How do practices get work from the PSA? Because of the size, complexity and duration of many of these jobs, one slightly disconcerting answer is that it often flows out of work they are already doing. For instance the naval training base at Gosport is like a small university town for 3000 sailors and their families. It called for a complete development plan over a 15-year period and a wide variety of building professionals are working on it. It was the result of the closing down of overseas bases, and Geoff Woodward makes the point that it's worth keeping an eye on government policy and indeed on political events if you want to get work from the PSA. "Changes of government have an effect, though because of the size and duration of projects it tends not to be an overnight one. On the other hand political events can make an immediate impact—think of the Falklands. That's a major source of PSA work at the moment."

In choosing new outside consultants a number of channels are used. One of the principal sources of information is a computerised list of firms compiled by the Directorate of Architecture and Quantity Surveying Services. It contains details of work they have done, partnership structure, location and so forth. In compiling that list the DAQSS liaise closely with the Clients' Advisory Service—in fact they use their classifications—and turn to them particularly for advice on architects for specialist and overseas work. The Director of Design Services keeps in continuous touch with what is happening on the architectural practice scene (for instance, he pays a good deal of attention to the professional press) and of course he receives a good many approaches these days from architects looking for work. He says, however, that it is far better to go in the first instance to the Director of Works in individual departments. Above all, he warns against merely sending a brochure or letter to the PSA at large in the hope that it will reach the right person. "You can't rely on that happening in a government organisation", he says and points out that an organisation chart of the PSA is published in their annual report. This is available from the PSA Public Relations Adviser, Room N 13/14, 2 Marsham Street, London SW1P 3EB.

Property Services Agency

The basis of selection is essentially one of horses for courses: the size of the office, its experience with the building type, site and location being considered, its record and the background of its partners are all factors to be taken into account. "You have to work hard at getting the right architect", he says. "It means talking to past clients, users of buildings he has designed and other consultants he has worked with. Success in competitions also has a bearing on things."

After that initial sifting process, they make a choice rather in the same way as any other client. "We ask firms to come in for an interview. We describe the project and generally set the scene for what's involved. They have to convince us that they're right for the job, not only in terms of their design ideas—how they would tackle the project—but also whether they have the staff and the experience to do it."

Once the choice of an outside architect is made, he is usually responsible for the whole job. There is no mixture of PSA and outside professionals, except that there is always a project manager who is always a PSA person. The architect, incidentally, is not necessarily the team leader or "lead professional" to use Woodward's term. It depends on the job content. "If a building has a high environmental design element the leader might be a consulting engineer. What we do stress however is that every consultant's duties stretch into every aspect of the work with which he's concerned. We don't believe things should be left to sub-contractors."

The PSA do, however, take charge over the division of fees—that is not left to the lead consultant. Woodward believes that the PSA will increasingly move towards some form of competitive fee tendering and his remarks were confirmed in an article in *Building Design* on 25.11.83. "There is likely to be a cut-off at £½ million for the cost of a project", the piece stated. "Over this the PSA will invite 'offers' from architects based on their design proposals." Woodward said that he did not believe this would give rise to a spate of cut-price work to the detriment of other considerations:

The Clients

It will be a question of seeing how many of the conditions of the architect's appointment can be fulfilled for a given fee, though there won't be any cutting of corners on quality. A lot of firms are already working on some such basis for private sector clients.

The PSA's massive clout as clients means that they are unlikely to have much difficulty in dictating the terms under which architects work with them, though they are also conscious of the importance of sustaining professional standards—and not just on the big prestige projects like overseas embassies. They are responsible for a fair amount of small-scale work at UK regional level and Woodward says that here they can be important clients for small local practices. It is worth keeping in touch, he believes, with the PSA's regional offices in places like Reading, Hastings, Bristol, Cardiff, Birmingham, Manchester, Leeds, Cambridge, and indeed the London regional office. As in the case of jobs emanating from PSA headquarters, they look at factors like track records, interesting buildings, magazine publicity and so forth. The bonus is that regional PSA contacts eventually lead to national ones, particularly if the architect in question makes sure that PSA's headquarters in Croydon get to hear of what he's doing at a regional level. "Dealing with government departments is like dealing with any other big organisation—you can't be sure that the good word will spread on its own."

Andrew Sutherland

We designed the house together—it was marvellous fun, like an elaborate game for grown-ups.

Andrew Sutherland (not his real name) is an example of that rare species, the genuine private client. Keenly interested in architecture and with enough money to finance his passion, he began his career as a client by commissioning a distinguished British architect to build him a house on a magnificent site he and his wife had acquired in Calabria. The distinguished architect declined the job because he felt that he would have to live near the site for a couple of months first to be able to do justice to it. He might also have had some inkling of the problems of dealing with local workmen which proved to be daunting even for the Italian architect he recommended—a man who had worked in his London office. Though he proved to be a better designer than a project manager, the relationship—and the house that resulted—was entirely successful.

Andrew Sutherland's next experience as a client was less happy. In this case the job was the major rehabilitation and adaptation of a house he had bought in St John's Wood. Speaking of it, he says, "Probably unconsciously the architect tried to impose her own taste and lifestyle on us. She pushed through a lot of ideas which were perfectly OK but which I didn't particularly like. I realised then that personal empathy was tremendously important, more so than reputation. The architect's job in that sense is to interpret the client's wishes in a buildable way—tell him what's possible and come up with something similar if it isn't, rather than impose a determinist solution about how the architect thinks the client ought to live."

He employed another architect on his next commission—a

The Clients

very extensive rehabilitation and partial reconstruction job on a Georgian house in north London. Here his criticism of the architect is one that in some degree or other is echoed by a great many clients—costs turned out to be much higher than the original estimates. "The place was in poor condition", he admits. "Some of the over-runs occurred because of unexpected problems with the fabric. But the architect also led me on a bit. In the course of the job he put forward much more expensive solutions than the ones he'd originally suggested, and of course that has a domino effect on other parts of the process." Sutherland feels that consciously or unconsciously architects have the idea that the client has much more money to spend than he says he has. "I was able to meet the additional costs because of an unexpected legacy, but if that hadn't been the case I would have been forced to sell, or go to the bank for a loan I might not necessarily have got."

Sutherland's spending capacity as a private client is comparatively small. However in his working existence he is an institutional patron of some importance. In that role he has chosen yet another architect who had done some excellent work for his former in-laws. He has discarded the two firms who had previously worked for him in the UK. The moral of that particular story is not lost on successful private sector architects like John Winter: it is that a relatively minor private client can, in another role, be an important institutional one, or can turn into one as he moves up the career ladder.

Trafalgar House Developments Ltd

A recommendation upwards from development managers and directors of subsidiary companies may be as effective as a direction downwards from me. The important thing is to pick the right team and actually to be able to get on with your opposite number.

Trafalgar House's network of associated companies is probably wider than that of any other developer. To name just two out of several in the building field alone, they include Trollope & Colls and Cementation. As developers they are among the two or three largest in the country, dealing mainly with offices, retail centres and industrial buildings. The scale of their operations and their great financial strength means that their workload has carried them through the recession, although more recently new commitments have been fewer in number than usual.

Perhaps for this reason, G. H. B. Carter, the managing director of this important part of the Trafalgar House empire, is one of the few clients who says he is now getting regular direct approaches from practices looking for work. "To be frank, I don't pay much attention to that sort of thing", he says. He is more interested in architects who come with a recommendation from some consultant he knows or who come to him with a site for which they have obtained planning permission. "We're always keen to be kept in the picture about new men and new practices and to hear of development possibilities. If we go ahead with a proposal that has come to us from the outside, we'll always involve the architect who made it in some way, even where we feel he's not the right one to design that particular building."

Carter says what impresses him least are brochures without adequate back-up. "They generally contain highly flattering photographs of buildings or, even worse, scheme designs for things which were never built and which suggest the sender is scratching around for work. What I can really use best are addresses of buildings, names of owners and of other professionals with whom the architect has worked. I like to go round and see these places, talk to users about whether the building works and get to know what the architect was like as a member of the team."

The sort of abilities he looks for in a practice are that they are a commercially minded organisation, skilled at securing planning permission, capable of producing quality designs and competent at running a job. "These aren't always to be found simultaneously within one practice, so we might divide the job up, not necessarily retaining the architect through its whole course", he explains. "We might just work with him for the conceptual design or that plus the planning consents. In the final stages of running the job, the leader of the team might be the contractor and the architect will be retained as the design consultant." Carter says that from the architect's point of view this is by no means an unfavourable arrangement. "Much of the fee is related to the earlier stages of the job anyway." At any rate he insists that Trafalgar House must remain in the driving seat. "We pick all the members of the team, paying particular attention to the choice of the QS."

Trafalgar House talk to several architects before making their choice, though the architect sometimes comes with the site, particularly when THD have taken over from a smaller developer who may already have made a commitment to employ a certain individual or practice. At the other end of the scale, THD may be putting up a design for a site in order to get planning permission.

Trafalgar House's methods do not lead them much towards "vanguard" architects. "As commercial developers we've got to put up buildings that are worth at least what they cost which doesn't necessarily rule out that they could also be an architectural statement." Trafalgar is very keen to commission buildings of high architectural quality, but value for money can never be overlooked.

Personalities are also very important in their dealings with architects. "The chemistry is very important. You can be a terrific architect, but if you can't get on with the development director at our end the results are likely to be fairly unhappy." Carter thinks some big practices lose sight of this important factor. "The senior partners get over-committed sometimes and they start delegating too much. They may not be careful enough in the more junior appointments in their own office." For this reason THD keep their golden eggs in a number of architectural baskets and look for interesting new faces all the time. Furthermore, not all their projects are of a size that requires the resources of the larger developers' architects. "We try to find the appropriate architect for each type of job. We wouldn't choose a big firm to handle a small development. It's worthwhile for even a small firm to get in touch with us—provided, of course, that they can show us that they can come up to our standards."

Part 3
The Intermediaries

Peter Davey: Editor of the Architectural Review

Paradoxically the architects I most respect are not primarily concerned to get their work published.

What Peter Davey means by that somewhat cryptic remark is that the architects he is most interested in are concerned with the quality of publication, not its mere fact. He goes on to say that such architects "tend to be very concerned about how their work is presented. We do try to respond to the architect's ideas of design and lay-out, but it's not always possible within the economics of magazine publishing." That comment touches on a central problem of quality specialist magazines like the AR. They have a limited circulation in comparison to glossies like, say, *House & Garden*, and that in turn imposes quite considerable production constraints. Yet architects expect their work to be illustrated as handsomely in the AR as it would be in a consumer magazine.

That, in a sense, is a tribute to the AR's continuing importance in the profession. It has been the leading British architectural monthly for the best part of a century. It has shaped opinions and made reputations. It would be hard to think of anyone who is anybody, in and around architecture, certainly in Britain and the Commonwealth who has not written for it or had their buildings illustrated in it. In spite of some fairly considerable ups and downs in its fortunes in recent years it could be said that having a building discussed or even shown in the AR is as important for an architect as it is for a writer to have his book reviewed in the *Times Literary Supplement*.

The Intermediaries

In view of this, it is not surprising that the AR is an immediate and obvious target for press releases on all kinds of aspects of architects' work—interior design as well as actual buildings. Only about one per cent of them are followed up as far as publication and indeed the majority get no further than the waste paper basket at editorial meetings. "Often they're not really presented in a form suitable for an architectural magazine", says Davey. "They're aimed at the property pages of newspapers or at features editors of general-interest glossies."

So what sort of material does attract his attention? Curiously enough, it need not be anything expensive or lavishly produced. "I like to see a good photo, but it needn't be professionally taken. I'm an architect myself, so I can see whether a building will make a piece without having to see a 'posed' photograph—though, of course, a consumer magazine might have different requirements. When we do finally show the building we would have professional photos made. I also like to see drawings, especially working drawings. With such material there should be a brief text, and what I'm interested in there is not just a description of the building, but the ideas behind it. As a quality architectural magazine we aim to publish buildings where the intellectual content and its visual expression form a stimulating unity." Davey says architects' own houses are often interesting in this way. "In fact," he adds, "there's wide general interest in the houses architects build for themselves and it's not just confined to professional magazines. I'd say that designing your own house is an excellent way of getting publicity."

Of course, even there the AR is pretty selective in what it publishes. "If you want to know what sort of buildings are apt to get published the best thing is to take out a subscription to the AR," he recommends. That would also clarify the confusion about what exactly the AR puts out in contrast to its stablemate, the weekly AJ. Sometimes the same building appears in both papers, but Davey insists that even then, the emphasis is different. "The AJ is about *how* you make things. The AR is about *what* you make. It's 'a state of the art' publication".

Sometimes architects come in to see him, though he prefers them to send material in advance and leave him the option of making an appointment. "That's how I came to publish the New Zealand architect Roger Walker. He sent in some pictures of the fascinating work he's doing in a sort of New Zealand vernacular based on the use of corrugated iron. He then came to see me when he was in London."

On the whole one gets the feeling that Davey likes to discover work for himself rather than have it forced on his attention. He travels around a good deal. "There's a feeling that editors don't stray outside London much, but that's not true, either of myself or my colleagues—and, indeed, competitors. We're always interested in good new work and we rely a good deal on word of mouth from reliable friends and contacts to hear about it." Exhibitions are also a source of such information and Davey makes a point of going to the main ones. He also follows the teaching circuit fairly closely. People who both build and teach tend to do interesting work and he holds a high opinion of teachers in general. "Of course it does depend a bit on where you teach", he admits. "I suppose at the moment the significant places, as far as the UK is concerned, are the AA, Cambridge, Glasow and Bath. Of course things can change very quickly. An influential teacher can make a school in a very short time—which is why it's important to keep one's tabs on them." Competitions are one of the most significant of all sources of material for a magazine like the AR—indeed they are now beginning to sponsor a few competitions of their own.

What about the view, held by some members of the profession, that specialist professional magazines like the AR are a declining force as a way of getting work, now that so much of it is coming from the private sector? Davey obviously rejects that. "There are definite advantages to being exposed to your professional peers", he says. "For instance professional opinion is often consulted when it comes to choosing firms to enter for limited competitions, and these are becoming increasingly important. I would think it's also useful in the context of the Clients' Advisory Service. And in the public sector—which still accounts for a large amount of work architects do and will continue to do so—jobs are handed out by civil service and local authority building professionals who go very much on what we and a few other magazines publish and have to say."

Leslie Fairweather: Editor of the Architects' Journal

Generally the most exclusive thing about an architectural story are plans and drawings. That's where you can really see how the architect has thought about the building. Anyone can go along and take a photograph.

The AJ has a weekly circulation of around 20,000 and a massive advertising revenue from manufacturers who recognise its status as the most influential magazine in the profession. But it does not hold that position without a constant challenge from its two formidable rivals, *Building* and *Building Design*. Advertisers, a hard-nosed lot not automatically impressed even by quasi-institutions like the AJ, need to be reassured that the magazine is read as well as seen. Consequently news value—and especially exclusive news stories, technical innovation and changes affecting the practice of architecture—are major factors Leslie Fairweather and his team of editors take into account in selecting publishable material from their daily post. Needless to say, that is immense. Getting into the AJ is something of an accolade and every day they receive a mixed bag of literally hundreds of letters, press releases about new buildings and schemes, invitations to publicity junkets and announcements about every conceivable kind of event that might be of interest to AJ readers.

Though the task of sorting through all this takes up a lot of time every morning, everything that comes in gets looked at. However, Fairweather shares the views of other editors about the poor quality of much of what comes in—especially press releases from architects and their PR firms. At the same time, he does not feel there is any particular mystique to getting it right. "More than anything else a press release about a building must say, in a few words, what the building is, who the architect is and what's different or special about it. Its particular interest may be technical or aesthetic, or even in the way it was financed—possibly a new way of solving a technical or contractual problem or a new approach to design. But there must be a reason to publish that building out of the many schemes and photos that are sent to us every week. Architects are very bad at putting over what that reason is."

Describing the selection process itself, Fairweather says that the obvious junk "goes straight into the waste paper basket". He tends to include under that heading not only the obviously irrelevant or sub-standard, but also approaches he finds off-putting. "I particularly dislike pointless booze-ups". If the editors—there are groups of editors who look after buildings, news, the technical section and practice—decide at the morning meeting that something looks interesting, they write or phone for more details. There are also meetings at which, "we decide what to do about the material that's been sent in, either as a follow-up to those enquiries or material we have requested about buildings known to us. The building or project might merit a captioned picture; or, next stage up, it might be worth a 2–3 page feature. The full treatment would be a building study of 16 pages or so, with detailed cost and energy analyses." All subsequent drawings and photographs (and that increasingly, these days, includes four colour) are prepared by AJ staff or by commissioned freelance draughtsmen and photographers.

Fairweather admits that the AJ tends to cover buildings by "stars" and "near-stars" and also that there are certain architects, whose work they know well and which they regard as almost continuously interesting, who will get fairly regular, though not guaranteed coverage. But, he says, he himself has no ideological bias, nor do he and the other

Leslie Fairweather: Editor of the Architects' Journal

editors slavishly follow whatever the latest architectural fashion might be. "We're interested in whatever is good of its kind", he says, "although obviously some editors are more dedicated to one particular direction than another, whether it be the modern movement or community architecture. Our group method of working should ensure that we achieve a fair balance. Appropriate design, soundly based practice, technical competence, and integrity towards both clients and society, are what the AJ is interested in promoting."

In accordance with that view the AJ has in recent years been increasingly involved in sponsoring competitions and awards and Fairweather particularly believes in the role of the Royal Academy in promoting good architecture to the public: "Last year, with the Towco Group (a firm of service engineers and contractors) we founded three awards for architecture with prize money of £5000, plus a bronze for the outright winner. The awards are given for exhibits in the architecture room at the RA Summer Show. There's a first prize for the finest design overall, which also communicates the architects' intentions best with the public. The second prize is for the most promising newcomer and we were very pleased that in 1983 it went to a recently qualified student. The third prize is for the best presented drawing or model as an art form in its own right. We're running the award scheme for at least five years to improve the quality and quantity of architecture shown at the Academy, and to help the public understand good design. We also run a £10,000 award with the Otis Elevator Company: winners in 1983 were the Covent Garden design team."

Another way to get publicity via the AJ is to be nominated as a freelance specialist contributor. There are several architects who have found this to be materially helpful in building up their practices: Jolyon Drury and Brian Waters, for instance, are among those discussed in this book. Although the AJ has a sizeable editorial team, they are always looking for new writers. "We're very interested in finding architects who can write well and authoritatively, and in

191

The Intermediaries

discovering new illustrators and photographers. These days, at a time when there are so many changes taking place in the profession, we're also interested in new approaches to traditional architectural practice, from community architecture at one end of the spectrum to the various forms of consultancy in our coverage of the practical aspects of running a practice. We're also very keen to publish anything that's new and relevant on computer applications for architects. In fact we run our own computer club to keep us in touch with developments and for the exchange of information."

The AJ's editors give an unusual amount of guidance to outside contributors on matters of writing and presentation style and content. But as for deciding whether what you want to say is of prima facie interest to the AJ, that is a matter of reading the magazine, looking at what it is doing and submitting proposals (*not* completed articles) relevant to that. It's a question of putting yourself in the editors' shoes—a principle of empathy that applies throughout to the process of getting and promoting work. Some people would call it marketing.

Peter Murray: Editor of the RIBA Journal

Every architectural paper is a bit different from the others. Above all, we're totally different from the consumer magazines and local papers most press releases are aimed at.

The big difference between the RIBA *Journal* and its competitors is that though it is extremely influential as the official journal of the Institute, the fact that it is sent out free to all the members means that it has to rely entirely on advertising revenue—not easy to get for a monthly magazine, even if it does have a controlled circulation of around 25,000. Murray cannot afford frills like expensive photographers' fees. "We have to rely on architects sending in good material and frankly what we get is often very poor", he says. "The usual thing is half a dozen pictures taken by the architect himself and a wodge of grey dyeline prints. We're very far from giving preference to the work of metropolitan architects, though of course we do have to cover the star names. But it's the quality of the illustrative material sent in that rules out a lot of otherwise interesting stuff." In addition to professionally taken pictures—or at least pictures approximating to professional standards—he likes to get A4 reductions rather than unwieldy dyeline prints.

The RIBA *Journal*, like the AJ and AR, is a target for dozens of press releases, but like the editors in Queen Anne's Gate, Murray says the vast majority are unusable. "The people who send them in, practices and PR firms—they at any rate should know better—often don't seem to have looked at the sort of thing RIBAJ publishes. The fact that the Queen is opening a new building designed by a particular firm is great for local papers, but it simply isn't the sort of item we run as a profession-oriented monthly."

The Intermediaries

At the same time there are opportunities to get publicity in the Journal which are going begging. For instance there is the "New Works" page for which Murray is eager to get news. He also says that he would like to see more suitable entries for the "Practice Pictorial" feature, though the pre-requisite is that the buildings should be interesting or the practice be doing something unusual.

"If you want to get material published in the RIBA *Journal*, the best advice I can give is to look at the sort of buildings and features that appear there. I can't point to any stylistic preferences of mine—I'm simply interested in good buildings, though like everyone else I find that hard to define. As far as feature articles are concerned, we do a number of special issues each year on topics like energy, new products, overseas work, or whatever happens to be a subject that we think needs a wider airing. These are announced in January and we are always looking for people who write in to us and who might have something interesting to say about them."

One reason why it is worth keeping in touch with Murray—though modestly it is not a point he makes himself—is that he is far more influential than his position suggests. He moved to the RIBA after an outstanding spell as editor of *Building Design* and he has recently become the independent publisher of what promises to be a prestigious new architectural journal—*Blueprint*. "We're looking for issues and fashions in architecture", is the way he explains *Blueprint*'s editorial policy. "But we prefer to pick these out for ourselves. It's a case of 'don't ring us, we'll ring you' ".

Deyan Sudjic: Architectural Correspondent, Sunday Times

The first hurdle is when you start. The next is after five years, particularly when you've made your name with a widely discussed building. That kind of project tends to absorb an enormous lot of time and energy, so that looking for new work gets put aside.

Over the last two or three years Deyan Sudjic has emerged as one of the journalists whose attention most architects doing anything important or innovative would like to catch. Though he writes regularly for the *Sunday Times*, his work also appears in places as diverse as *Cosmopolitan*, *The World of Interiors* and *Time Out*. He is among the pioneers of a new style of architectural criticism and comment that is concerned with fashion and what the Americans call "lifestyle" rather than the heavier end of "architects writing about architecture for other architects"—as some traditional architectural journalism has been described. Because of that approach he looks for buildings that exemplify a style or a trend as much as work that is interesting in itself, and he divides his very prolific output into three main areas: features, which are criticisms of individual buildings, news stories ("often bad news about something an architect has done", he says), and longer magazine pieces about buildings, projects or individuals.

Like other architectural writers and editors he gets lots of press releases and handouts, most of which are unuseable.

"The worst stuff comes from big PR firms who have no idea of how to present architecture. All I want in the first instance is a couple of good pictures and a couple of good descriptive paragraphs", he says. "If the building sounds interesting, I'm quite tempted by some kind of official opening or viewing. For a journalist that kind of occasion means that you have to do something about it, or the competition will get the story. Otherwise one tends to put off looking at a building until some convenient day—which may be a long way off."

Sudjic is himself a trained architect, and one of his main sources of information is the professional press. For instance, he was prompted to follow up and write about Campbell Zogolovitch Wilkinson & Gough's housing designs in Hackney after reading Andrew Saint's article about it in the AJ. He also keeps an eye on RIBA Awards and other similar signs of public recognition; and like other architecture watchers he has noted the growing tendency for important work to be exhibited at the Royal Academy Summer Show.

But like all journalists he relies most of all on a grapevine of friends, contacts and gossip through which the often mysterious process of making news and establishing reputations is transacted. How exactly a name suddenly becomes well-known is hard to pin down though. Nobody had heard of Eva Jiricna a couple of years ago and Terry Farrell's name was known primarily only to other architects. Today you can hardly open a magazine with a design feature that does not contain their work or some mention of it. "Finding the right job and the right client is very important", Sudjic says, in trying to explain what happens. "Eva Jiricna's name came to the fore because she did a job for Joseph Ettudgi, a very publicity-conscious client. Terry Farrell became widely known because Peter Jay and David Frost commissioned him to do the TV/AM studios and of course that was an event that was surrounded by an enormous lot of news coverage." Good connections at the right time are very important, too. The CZWG partners were friends of Janet and Tim Street-Porter's while they were still at the AA: two people with a very high profile in the younger end of the media establishment.

The crucial thing in starting up a practice, Sudjic thinks, is to choose your first jobs and clients with great care— assuming, as he puts it, that you want to be a consultant, not a GP. "In the nature of things, though, most architects who want to set up on their own want to do so because they want to be a consultant—in the sense, that is, that they want to make a personal statement. Quite often that goes with a highly individualistic personal style as well, like Cedric Price's cigar and stiff white collar or Peter Cook's green spectacles. The problem is that fashion changes and that you get typecast. That can be very dangerous for some bright young firms."

What happens in such cases? "Some of them simply lose their inspiration and turn out the same buildings as everyone else", he says. "But that isn't as safe as it used to be, because clients are getting more sophisticated. The day of the commercial architect turning out routine competent stuff is by no means over—but playing safe is not the invariably right answer that it was ten years ago." The ones who last have the capacity to change and adapt. "One of the things I admire about Jim Stirling is that he keeps on trying to do something new and also that he keeps bringing new blood into the practice."

The other way is to identify what you're really good at and to concentrate on that. Sudjic quoted DEGW as a good example. "They had very little work for a long while but they continued building up their reputation as space planners by writing and lecturing instead of going off in some other direction. Now new work is rolling in because the whole office design scene is being revolutionised and they're feeding back to their clients the expertise in space planning that they went on acquiring during their lean years."

Ultimately, though, there are no prescriptions for the kind of success that makes an architect a name that anyone outside the profession has heard of or that journalists will seek out. Probably, as in the other arts, architecture is a calling in which few are ever chosen in that sense.

Peter Sandy: RIBA Clients' Advisory Service

Many architects don't understand marketing. They think it's something vaguely unprofessional that smacks of "selling yourself". But all it really means is responding to clients' needs and understanding their problems.

Although the Clients' Advisory Service is the RIBA's principal official work-generating arm for its members it has to be said that a great many of the practices interviewed in connection with this book were highly critical about its effectiveness. Certainly this was the case with the smaller, less established ones. Some said it was an institutionalised old-boy network, at any rate as far as the larger, more desirable jobs were concerned. Others said you could get work through it if you badgered them sufficiently. One frequent source of criticism was that it did not vet client enquiries and match them intelligently with practices on the register. For instance Cedric Price actually asked his name to be removed from it because he considered that the jobs he was being offered through CAS were wildly unsuitable. "My name was put forward to design a showroom for a firm producing pastiche 18th-century furniture, because I'd done some furniture showrooms—but for modern furniture. There's nothing I'd like to do less than to design an environment for fake antiques."

As against that, there are practices who say that leads from CAS are what you make of them. Hulme Chadwick, for instance, have lately won a refurbishment job with a contract value of £1m which began as an enquiry to CAS about the redesign of an entrance hall and display area. It turned into a study of wider options open to the client from which this much larger assignment emerged.

Peter Sandy, recently appointed to run CAS, says that quite a number of jobs come about through a CAS introduction but are never attributed to this. He wants to correct that by publicising major CAS achievements through the RIBA *Journal*. This, however, is only part of a much larger plan to step up the Service's activities and heighten awareness among both members and clients about what it can do.

In the past the constraints on marketing imposed by the Code forced it to play a somewhat passive role as a clearing house for information about practices. There are, of course, valuable aspects to that which they want to carry on with. "We maintain a computerised file of practices who have registered with us, indexed by expertise in particular building types, skills, location, projects done and so forth. We also hold documentation such as practice brochures to back up that information. Then, when a client enquiry for an architect to do a particular kind of job comes in, we send the client a list of suitable names. Regional and branch chairmen are also involved in the selection process for all but the most insignificant jobs and our lists are always referred to the RIBA President on contract values of over £3m. In so far as qualitative judgements are made at all, they are made via an RIBA member elected by his or her peers. The final choice, of course, is left to the client. CAS merely acts as a marriage bureau."

Sandy would like CAS to be more of a marriage broker as well. He divides the market between corporate clients like IBM and the big developers, the public sector and private clients. The latter account for about a third of the construction market—in money terms £4 billion a year. "Some of that is small stuff", he concedes. "But there are a large number of substantial clients who have been influenced by the bad press architects have had in the last few years; and if not that, then they are uncertain about what an architect can actually do for them. It's our prime objective to correct that by convincing the private sector in particular that the Clients' Advisory Service can provide solid professional guidance which will also be disinterested—except in so far as we want them to use architects to solve their building problems."

One of the steps the Clients' Advisory Service has taken to help broaden the client base is to appoint a consultant who is not an architect, but who has wide experience of the construction industry as a whole: Peter Trollope, formerly a senior executive with his family firm, Trollope and Collis. He and Peter Sandy visit about six practices a week to advise them on marketing problems. They would also like to provide a more general marketing service to the profession and to individual practices—for instance to offer market research into trends and opportunities. They are keen to promote the idea that good design is value for money, by such steps as organising exhibitions and seminars at Chambers of Commerce, through the CBI and through other influential client bodies.

"The trouble is that we can only go at the speed and scale at which we're funded by members", says Sandy. At the moment most of the CAS's income is from expanded entries in the Directory of Practices, but he would like to boost that by making a small charge for entry into the CAS Practice Index, and a further charge, related to contract value, for jobs which come to practices through a CAS introduction. Ideally, but perhaps controversially, he would also like to charge a consultancy fee to clients who come to CAS for advice.

He is critical about the way some architects respond to clients' enquiries. "Pointing out the quality of work done in the past is fine as far as it goes, but it's not enough", he says. "You have to show that you can really respond to clients' needs and understand their problems. That process begins right at the practice switchboard with answering calls in a prompt and efficient manner. In the course of the job it means having a firm grasp on the client's principal problems and their solution—time, money, ability to programme the work or whatever."

Shortcomings in these respects were one of the factors to emerge in a survey CAS conducted about why architects recommended to clients were not appointed; or, having been appointed, were not satisfactory.

The main complaint was that they didn't have an adequate grasp of commercial realities. That doesn't mean they weren't appointed because they refused to be developers' hacks. It means that clients felt they didn't really exhibit an adequate interest in what the client's main concerns were likely to be—like the importance of getting finished within a certain time.

There was a very similar reason for unhappiness with architects' performance once the job was under way. "The client wants to know whether the building will be finished by a certain date. You can't just say, as some architects do, 'you'll have to ask the contractor'. That's tantamount to an admission that you haven't got a grip of the situation." Sandy in fact sees the future role of the architect as being an ambitious and wide-ranging one, extending to the management of all resources to do with building and development as well as close control of the building process itself.

One problem, though it was not one that he himself voiced, may be the JCT contract, which places too much power in the hands of contractors. More fundamentally, though the one does not exclude the other, it is that the designer–builder relationship is at fault, and that is part of a historical process of attitude formation. "There's been a long tendency for architects to think of themselves as 'artists' and 'professionals' who leave the business of actually organising the work to the horny-handed contractor. As we all know, for contractual case law reasons an adversarial relationship has built up, in which all parties try to protect themselves amid the small print, instead of working together."

Trying to correct that situation and to set up better relationships between all parties in the building process—in the first instance by sending out questionnaires to try and identify the problems—is one important part of Sandy's mission. Another is to try and standardise—and improve—the brochures and other material architects send in to CAS. "Not only is much of it no good—despite the fact that hours of partner time have been directed into it—but it's all shapes and sizes and methods of presentation. What is wanted is a record divided up by building types, with information on job sizes, clients, location and so forth—not a lot of verbiage, just the information the client needs to have in the first instance." The role of CAS, he says, is essentially that of an active interface based on records of what the practice has done, research into what the client wants and promotion of the practice based on that knowledge.

Sandy sees RIBA competitions as a natural extension of that process. "As far as clients are concerned the question to be considered is whether a competition will really reach the objectives he's generally after. Then you go on to develop a brief that will fine-tune that to meet quite specific needs." Sandy thinks that competing on price will eventually be controlled by the conditions of the architect's appointment. "Clients will be made to appreciate that what matters is that range of services the fee will buy, and that a corner-cutting attitude from the outset is unlikely to produce a good building", he thinks.

Peter Sandy is under no illusions that educating architects to market themselves will be an easy process. "Buildings don't speak for themselves—they only speak to other architects. Clients—even happy clients—forget about you very quickly. Every practice should allocate five to fifteen per cent of its income to marketing. That doesn't just mean promotion, market research and attractive presentation. It will mean—we hope—fully supporting new initiatives at CAS, though of course it also extends to taking care of quite ordinary things, such as keeping the bits the client sees clean and polished. That, in turn, involves everything from having the office look organised, with decent furniture and equipment, to seeing that the job architect turns up on time to meetings."